Christian Home

A Guide to Happiness in the Home

Rev. Fr. Celestine Strub, O.F.M.

If the social reform that is being demanded on
all sides is to have any hope of success, it must
begin with the reform of the family.
—Victor Cathrein, S.J.

ANGELUS PRESS
2918 TRACY AVENUE, KANSAS CITY, MISSOURI 64109

Nihil Obstat

Fr. Conradin Walbraum, O.F.M.
Censor Dep.
Fr. Liberatus Presser, O.F.M.
Censor Dep.

J.F. Green, O.S.A.
C.L.
April 7, 1934

Imprimi Permittitur
Fr. Optatus Loeffler, O.F.M.
Min Prov.
Die2 Martii, 1934

Imprimatur
George Cardinal Mundelein
April 7, 1934

To Christian Fathers and Mothers,
Husbands and Wives
and to all home-lovers the world over
this little volume is affectionately dedicated
under the patronage of the
supreme models of the Christian Home,
Jesus, Mary, and Joseph.

ANGELUS PRESS

2918 TRACY AVENUE
KANSAS CITY, MISSOURI 64109
PHONE (816) 753-3150
FAX (816) 753-3557
ORDER LINE 1-800-966-7337

ISBN 0-935952-30-6
Angelus Press Second Printing—December 1995

Printed in the United States of America

Introduction

THE world to-day is full of reformers. Society, we are told, is sick with many ills, and a radical remedy is imperative if the utter breakdown of Christian civilization is to be averted. Yet, while the urgent need of reform is quite generally conceded, there is a wide divergence of opinions as to the proper means of bringing it about. As Catholics, possessed of the divinely revealed truths that should regulate all human action, we know that many of the remedies proposed for the cure of social ills are inadequate, because they do not reach the root of the evil; and that many a well-meant reform movement is foredoomed to failure, because it is not based on the only true and solid foundation of all social reform; namely, the principle that there can be no real, permanent social justice and morality without private justice and morality; and that there can be no enduring private justice or morality without religion.

A Truism

So much is agreed upon among Catholics: religion and morality must form the basis of all true reform; and it is a truism to say that if all the individuals that make up society were morally good and religious, the ills that afflict society would disappear. It is furthermore agreed among Catholics that the Catholic Church offers the individual all that is necessary for leading a good life. Why then do

3

so many of her children fail? They have the true
Faith; they have the Commandments, which tell
them what they must do and what they must avoid;
and they have the means of grace, prayer and the
Sacraments, to help them to avoid sin and practice
virtue. Why, then, are they not all morally good
and religious?

The Sin of Adam

The fundamental reason is simply that they do
not choose to be so. Sin is apparently so pleasant,
at least for the moment, and the constant practice
of virtue is so hard, that men often choose the
former in preference to the latter. Even in Paradise, where all circumstances were so favorable,
Adam and Eve abused their free will by disobeying
God. But in consequence of that first sin of Adam,
there exists in all his descendants a strong inclina-
tion to evil, which makes the practice of virtue still
more difficult. And added to all this is the example of the wicked world in which we live.

The Enemy Without

It is this latter, the bad example of the world
around us, which forms the great obstacle to social
reform even among Catholics. If man were merely
an individual living by himself, he would have only
the enemy within to fight against; but being a social
being, destined by God to live in society with others,
he has also an enemy outside himself—the evil example of many of those with whom he lives. How
to overcome this evil example is the great problem

of social reform. It is easy enough to say that the bad example must be offset by good example; but how and where is the good example to be had?

Catholic Societies

Many there are who say that since it is mainly social attractions that lead Catholics into dangerous company and dangerous places of amusement, we must have our own societies, our own social agencies, club rooms and recreation centers, so that our people can satisfy their craving for company and amusement in a harmless manner. While admitting that our people should be provided with ample opportunity for healthful and innocent recreation; while admitting, too, the importance and desirability of Catholic societies, both secular and religious, and attesting that, when properly conducted under proper auspices, such societies can do an immense amount of good, I am nevertheless of the opinion that it is not by means of these societies that social evils will be greatly reduced. Let us have these societies by all means; but when we have established them and made them flourish, let us not imagine that our task is done. In all such societies something is wanting,—namely, the intimate daily association of the members in all the important affairs of life.

The Best Catholic Society

Happily, however, there is a society that has this all-important requisite; a natural society in which the great majority of men spend their lives; a society that is capable of exerting a lifelong influence on its members. That society, dear reader, is the family. In the family we have all the essential things that man requires as a social being for his physical, moral and intellectual well-being and advancement. And since the family rather than the individual, is the unit of society, to reform society one must begin with the family. Restore religion to its rightful place in the home; let religion direct, control and permeate the family life, and not only will the individual have the safeguard he needs against the evils of society, but society itself will be transformed. This, then, religion in the home, is to my mind, the best of all remedies for the reform of society; and the purpose of this little book is to explain the remedy and to induce all Christian families that can be reached to adopt it.

"For the love of our Savior, Jesus Christ, we implore pastors of souls, by every means in their power, by instructions and catechisms, by word of mouth and by written articles widely distributed, to warn Christian parents of their grave obligations. And this should be done not in a merely theoretical and general way, but with practical and special application to the various responsibilities of parents touching the religious, moral, and civil training of their children, and with indication of the methods best adapted to make their training effective, supposing always the influence of their own exemplary lives."—Pius XI, "Christian Education of Youth."

CHAPTER I

Necessity of Religion in the Home

I

Primary End of the Family

IN accordance with the words spoken by God to our first parents, "Increase and multiply and fill the earth," the primary purpose of the family is the propagation of the human race. Now without religion, this purpose will be only imperfectly attained. All history witnesses to the fact that there can be no enduring morality without religion, and the history of the family is no exception to the rule. The suffering and labor, the difficulty and disappointment, the grief and vexation incident to the bearing and rearing of children demand so much patience, love, and self-sacrifice, that no one not imbued with a religious sense of duty and buoyed up by the hope of an eternal reward, will be willing to endure them. Hence where these religious motives are wanting, the primary end of the family will be either wholly or partly neglected, and matrimony degraded to the low level of a selfish partnership or a sinful pastime.

Perverting Marriage

We need not have recourse to pagan lands, where infants are deliberately exposed to die, for proof that such is the inevitable result of the absence of religion in the family. The absence or scarcity of children in many families of our own land is sad and sufficient evidence. Nay, even in Christian families, where religion no longer exerts the sway it should, are found those immoral practices that pervert the sublime aim of the family. One might, and in charity one would be bound to, ascribe the absence or scarcity of children in such families to other causes, if wives and mothers did not openly advocate artificial restriction of families on the theory that it is better to have one or two children and bring them up well than to have a larger number and be unable to take proper care of them. That theory in itself, of course, is unassailable so long as no law of God is violated by having only one or two children, and so long as the expression "proper care" is rightly understood. But just the way this theory is understood and put into practice by most of its advocates shows into what errors man falls when he is not restrained by the salutary curb of religion.

Educating for Heaven

What is meant by bringing up a child well? From the standpoint of religion, as far as essentials are concerned, it means to bring up a child in such a manner that it will be enabled to attain the end for which God created it—eternal happiness in Heaven. Such an education even the poorest parents will be able to provide for their children, no matter how many they have; and their own happiness in Heaven will be increased by every child that they have added to the number of the elect. There is always a possibility of a child going wrong

despite the best parental care; but the probability
of its going wrong from neglect because of the
large number of children is far less than the probability that it will be spoiled if it is one of a limited
few. The very action of the parents in thwarting
nature by limiting their offspring will militate
against the proper religious training of their children; for it is not likely that parents who themselves disobey the law of God in so grave a matter
will be at great pains to rear God-fearing sons and
daughters.

"Proper Care" Relative

But even from a material point of view, the as-
sumption is false that parents cannot take proper
care of many children. "Proper care" is to be
understood relatively, not absolutely; for while
parents are bound to provide for the material as
well as the spiritual needs of their children, the
extent of that provision must vary with the parents'
resources. If the best possible training and the best
possible care were required for every child, few
persons would be allowed to marry at all; since few,
if any, could be found whose circumstances could
not be improved on.

Periodic Continence

If really serious financial straits or imperative
considerations of health should discountenance the
addition of another child to the family at a given
time, truly Christian parents will know how to meet
the situation by mutually agreeing to practice con-

Pope Pius XI on the Rearing of Children

"We are deeply touched by the sufferings of those parents who, in extreme want, experience great difficulty in rearing their children. However, they should take care lest the calamitous state of their external affairs should be the occasion for a much more calamitous error. No difficulty can arise that justifies the putting aside of the law of God which forbids all acts intrinsically evil. There is no possible circumstance in which husband and wife cannot, strengthened by the grace of God, fulfill faithfully their duties and preserve in wedlock their chastity unspotted."

—Encyclical on Christian Marriage.

tinence over a certain period. So much, with a good will and God's grace, they will always be able to do. But no combination of untoward circumstances can ever justify the misuse of the sacred rights of marriage.*

I realize most keenly that faithful adherence to the law of God will sometimes require great sacrifices of God-fearing parents. But every state of life, as it confers certain rights and privileges, also demands its peculiar sacrifices; and God will always grant sufficient grace to enable one to make them. If God enables those husbands and wives to keep His holy law who are deprived of the legitimate pleasures of wedlock by the premature death or the life-long illness of their spouses, He will certainly do the same for those whom poverty or other trying conditions place in a similar predicament. With St. Paul, every Christian can say in time of trial: "I can do all things in Him that strengtheneth me."

An Extreme Case

The following example, which is about as extreme a case as one might imagine, shows how God strengthens and consoles those sorely tried consorts who place their trust in Him. I condense the story narrated by the chief actor himself—an English Catholic journalist named W. Gerald Young—in a letter to the London Universe.

"Some years ago I stood with a woman at the altar where God united us in the bonds of holy Matrimony. She was all that man could wish for, and, with her, life was a succession of sunny days.

---

*See quotation on opposite page.

More than once did God give her that wonderful blessing of radiant motherhood, and we were intensely happy. Today, however, black clouds of sorrow have overwhelmed us, and we are no longer together.

"Once a week I make a pilgrimage into the beautiful hill country of Surrey, where there is an institution known by the name of a mental hospital. Here it is that my dear one spends her days,—long, weary days, because she is mad. Here is my shrine. Frail and pallid, she lies on a bed, dead to the world of intelligence. Her once beautiful face is now disfigured; her old-time smile superseded by a scowl. When I kiss her dear lips, there is no warm response from the woman who loved me so dearly; and yet she still holds the keys of my heart.

"My journey back to London is a weary one; for how can we call it home when the wife and mother is absent? Little voices will ask when Mama is coming back, and Daddy cannot tell them. On my way back, I visit a little church wherein the Blessed Sacrament is always exposed for adoration. In this haven of rest where all is quiet and peaceful, I lift up my weary heart to God and tell Him my troubles, and I come out a happier man, because I have unburdened my soul to my Maker and He has given me new courage to fight this weary battle of life. Some day God may see fit to answer my petition. In the meantime I can only hope and pray." But whether God grants this brave man's prayer here on earth or not, oh, how magnificently will He reward his fidelity in eternity!

A Selfish Life

Now if a man can be faithful to the law of God in such trying circumstances, how much easier should it be for those whose happy homes are still unbroken and who need only practice Christian self-restraint? The whole argument against large families only shows the absence of the salutary restraints of religion. At bottom it is not the desire to give their children a more excellent training but the desire to lead a more selfish and comfortable life that clamors for the unnatural limitation of the family. No one is more desirous of having well-trained children than deeply religious parents; but such parents, regarding their office in the light of Faith, are bent mainly on rearing their children for Heaven; and they understand that, even should they be able to provide them but scantily with the goods of this world, by training them for Heaven the main thing is achieved and their principal duty performed. They realize, too, that the success of all their efforts in behalf of their children depends mainly on Heaven's blessing, and that if they merit that blessing by their upright lives, He who feeds the birds of the air and clothes the lilies of the field will also provide for their children.

Consolations of Parenthood

Happy the parents who still retain this religious outlook on life; whose religion is their guide, their support, and their consolation amid the arduous duties of their state of life! They know that they are the chosen instruments of Divine Providence for peopling the abode of the blessed. They know that in assuming the office of parenthood, they co-operate with God himself in bringing into existence beings destined to praise and enjoy Him forever in Heaven. They know that every child they receive is a gift of God; since, do what they will, they can have no child that God does not give them. But above the solace of all this knowledge, is the supernatural aid which the true religion affords them. They have the actual graces of the sacrament of Matrimony, of frequent Communion, and of daily prayer to strengthen them, and the example of their suffering Savior to console them. Yes, with religion in their homes, they can resist the evil example of those godless couples who seek only their own gratification. And though eugenic wise-acres scoff, and even misguided friends smile in derision at their old-fashioned families, they will never thwart Heaven's designs concerning their families, but look upon every child as a new token of Heaven's trust and Heaven's love.

The Parents' Pride

It is remarkable how often God rewards parents of large families by making the children that came last become the chief joy and pride of their life. The Little Flower of Jesus was the last of nine children; St. Ignatius of Loyola, the thirteenth; and St. Catherine of Siena, the twenty-fourth or twenty-fifth. Many parents owe the honor of having a son raised to the priesthood to the fact that they had large families. Had my own parents been willing to have five children but no more, they would never have had a priest in the family. But because they were blessed with eight children, they had the happiness of seeing the sixth and seventh celebrate their first Mass on the same day; and though they have gone to their reward, they are no doubt happy to know that two sons of their eighth child are studying for the priesthood.

A few years ago, I received a letter from a young mother of two children, in which she related how certain worldly-wise women try to induce mothers to limit the number of their children. On the occasion of a social call, a lady acquaintance of hers had remarked: "It is not a woman of refinement nowadays that has more than two children." To which the young mother replied: "In that case I hope to belong to the common herd, as I intend to take all that the good Lord wants to give me." In replying to her letter, I commended her for her truly Catholic stand, and then added: "I thank God that my own good mother did not have such a false idea of refinement; for if she had, I should have had no chance at all, as I was her seventh child." And the very first time I related this incident, namely, to a group of Franciscan Fathers at St. Elizabeth's Friary, Denver, Colo., each one of the *five* priests present declared that he, too, was his mother's seventh child!

II

Final Aim of Marriage

Necessary as religion is in the home for the attainment of the primary aim of marriage and the family—the propagation of the human race, it is equally necessary for the attainment of the family's final aim—the education of children for Heaven. Above all else it is the soul of the child for which parents will have to render a strict account on the day of judgment; and it is the religious and moral training of their children, therefore, that constitutes their paramount duty to their offspring. When Catholic parents stand before their Divine Judge, they will not be asked whether they did their utmost to enable their children to prosper in this world—to wear the laurels of its honors, to reap the fruits of its riches, and to quaff the wine of its sensual pleasures. No; the question they will have to answer is, whether they did their duty in enabling their children not only to save their immortal souls, but also to reach that degree of holiness to which God destined them and to embrace that state of life in which God wished them to serve Him.

Before the Dawn of Reason

To acquit themselves of this sacred duty, parents must needs foster religion in their home. If religion is to be planted deep in the heart of the child,—so deep that it will defy all later attempts of the world, the flesh and the devil, to root it out, it will not do to defer the child's religious education until it starts to school. Its religious education must be begun not only at the first dawn of reason, but long before the dawn of reason—in very infancy, so that a truly religious mind will be developed and become a veritable second nature. It follows necessarily, then, that religion must exert the dominant influence in the place where the child's first years are spent; namely, in the home. Religion should surround the child as snugly as its infant clothing. The child should imbibe religion at its mother's breast. It should be rocked to sleep to the tune of religion, and its first lisping accents should have a religious character. Only if religion rules the home, will the child get the impression right at the start that religion is the most important thing in life. If there is little or no religion in the home, the child will naturally be led to suppose that wealth and position, secular knowledge and training, or even worldly comforts and pleasures are the things most worth while; and that religion, instead of being a vital force in life, is merely a polite concession that man feels he must occasionally make to God, his Creator; and hence that it is, like a badge or his best clothes,—to be displayed only in church and on special occasions.

Religion a Spiritual Food

Few parents who send their children to a Catholic school will deny the necessity of religion in the school. They know that even if a school should be entirely non-sectarian and in no way opposed to religion, the mere absence of religion would itself

be a great evil; for, if education means the training
and instructing of a child for the performance of
the duties of life, it must needs embrace religious
training and instruction, since the practice of
religion is the first and foremost of life's duties.
Now what is true of the absence of religion in the
school, is equally true of its absence in the home.
The supernatural graces which the child received in
Baptism, sanctifying grace and the infused virtues
of Faith, Hope, and Charity, are awaiting nourishment and warmth in order to blossom forth and
yield fruit; and to deny the child the religious food
and atmosphere it craves is to stunt if not to
thwart its spiritual growth. To say that no harm
is done the child so long as it is taught nothing
positively bad or irreligious, is just as false as to
say that it will not harm a child to deprive it of
food so long as you do not give it poison.

Yet great as is the need of religion in the home
for the proper molding of the infant mind and
heart, how frequently is the hungry little soul of the
child practically starved until it begins to attend a
Catholic school! How often, too, is it not taught
things that are positively bad either by word or by
example! How often are not things said or done or
permitted in the presence of children and justified
or excused with the remark that "they don't know
what it means," or "it won't do them any harm"!
It may do them incalculable harm. It is just this seed
sown in the innocent child's memory and imagination, from which later on evil will spring; and then
the astonished parents wonder where the child

learnt it. Small children are the most impression-able beings in the world, and the impressions which they receive are the ones that sink deepest and that will leave their traces all through life.

Shifting the Burden

One reason why the child's religious education is often neglected at home, is the tendency on the part of parents to disemburden themselves of the duty of educating their children by committing that task entirely to others. The Catholic parochial school is unquestionably a splendid as well as a necessary institution; but it must be remembered that the education of children is in the first place the duty of the parents, and that the purpose of the school is only to co-operate with the parents, and in particular to take up the work at that point where the parents are no longer able to accomplish it satisfactorily themselves. That point, I am inclined to think, is ordinarily not reached before the child completes its sixth year, since there are few parents who are unable, from lack of either time or knowledge, to teach their children all they need to know on entering the first grade. There is, however, a growing custom of anticipating that point by entrusting the child to others when it is only five, or even only three or four years old; and the cause of the custom is the existence of the kindergarten.

Kindergarten vs. Home Training

There are those that favor the kindergarten; and it is easy to understand that, like the day nursery,

The Holy Father on the Decline of Family Education

"We wish to call your attention in a special manner to the present-day lamentable decline in family education. The offices and professions of a transitory and earthly life, which are certainly of far less importance, are prepared for by long and careful study; whereas for the fundamental duty and obligation of educating their children, many parents have little or no preparation, immersed as they are in temporal cares.

"The declining influence of domestic environment is further weakened by another tendency prevalent almost everywhere to-day, which, under one pretext or another, for economic reasons, or for reasons of industry, trade or politics, causes children to be more and more frequently sent away from home even in their tenderest years."

—Pius XI in "Christian Education of Youth."

it is a most welcome institution to mothers who are obliged to work away from home for the support of their families. While the use of the kindergarten in such a case is certainly above criticism, the same cannot be said in regard to its use by those parents who avail themselves of it merely to have the children off their hands. And, even where there is no lack of parental love and care, there is likelihood that parents will send their children to the kindergarten simply because others do so; or from the mistaken notion that they are supposed to do so. Now, without wishing to dogmatize in the matter, I want to tell such parents that, in my opinion, the kindergarten training is not superior to home training; and that nothing is learned in the kindergarten that cannot be learned equally well at home. It is quite true that the school mistress who specializes in her work may be intellectually better equipped than many mothers for the education of very young children; but it is none the less true that the mother is by nature the child's first and chief educator; that the mother is nature's own specialist just in the task of educating the child before it reaches the age of reason; and that, as regards religious training, it is every mother's bounden duty to acquire so much knowledge as will enable her to teach her children that rudimentary religious knowledge that they should have before they complete their sixth year.*

A Work of Love

Yet it is not so much duty, young mothers, that

---

*See quotation on opposite page.

I would emphasize, as love, to induce you to make the early education of your children your own personal task. Soon enough, yes all too soon the time will come when your darlings will pass from the sacred sanctuary of your home to spend the greater part of their waking hours elsewhere. Should your mother's love not be anxious to have them under your watchful eye as long as possible? During those first half dozen years, when the child's heart can be molded like soft clay, should you not desire to fashion it to the highest ideals with your own loving hands? Should you not wish to be able to say that those essential prayers, which you expect your children to recite daily through life, were first learned and lisped at their mother's knee? Should you not aim to bind them to their home by the strongest ties of interest as well as of affection? If so, then the surest way is to make the home the fountain at which they first drink the waters of wisdom; to make the home the attractive center of all their earthly hopes and joys and the holy shrine round which will caressingly cling the fondest of all the happy memories of childhood.

Harmony between School and Home

But even when parents have done all in their power for the religious education of their children before the latter begin to attend school, let them not imagine that their task is accomplished. When they finally commit them to the charge of others, at the proper age, they do not thereby divest themselves of all responsibility, but must co-operate with the teachers by their interest, their discipline, and their moral support.* Here again appears the necessity of religion in the home. If the child learns at school that it is in this world to serve God and to save its immortal soul, and that the things of earth are to be used merely as means to that end, that lesson must have an echo in the home. What the school emphasizes as the most important thing in life must likewise be regarded as such in the home. It will not do for the child to find a disagreement between the religious truths it learns at school and the views it hears expressed and defended at home. The irreconcilable opposition between the maxims of Christ and the maxims of this world will come home to the child soon enough; and if the former are to take root in its heart as they should, the seed sown in religious instruction in school must be nurtured by religion in the home.

A Puzzling Contradiction

It is true, the child will come in touch with irreligion sooner or later outside the circle of the home and school; but that is not likely to affect it so easily, since it has been taught to look upon the world as hostile to its own best interests. It will be quite different if irreligion is met with in the home. A child implicitly trusts its parents. It believes that they have its welfare at heart; and it will be confronted with a puzzling contradiction if its parents by word, deed, or omission countenance or counsel anything that it was taught at school to regard as wrong. Just because of its confidence in its parents, the

*See words of Holy Father on following page.

Pius XI on the Status of the School

"Since, however, the younger generations must be trained in the arts and sciences for the advantage and prosperity of civil society, and since the family of itself is unequal to this task, it was necessary to create that social institution, the school. But let it be borne in mind that this institution owes its existence to the initiative of the family and of the Church, long before it was undertaken by the State. Hence, considered in its historical origin, the school is by its very nature and institution subsidiary and complementary to the family and the Church It follows logically and necessarily that it must not be in opposition to, but in positive accord with those other two elements, and form with them a perfect moral union, constituting one sanctuary of education, as it were, with the family and the Church. Otherwise it is doomed to fail of its purpose and to become instead an agent of destruction."

—Encyclical on "Christian Education of Youth."

child is more likely to follow the example of the home than the precept it learned at school. Example is always more powerful than precept; and it is of the highest importance, therefore, that the religious instruction of the school be seconded by the example of sterling Christian conduct in the home. Only when home and school work hand in hand, mutually supporting, complementing, and encouraging each other, may we hope that our children will receive the kind of education that will enable them to bring forth the fruits of a truly Christian life.

Non-Catholic Schools Forbidden

The very fact that the school is supposed to continue the education of the home and that both must be pervaded by the same Christian spirit, shows the obligation that Catholic parents are under of placing their children only in a Catholic school. In his encyclical on the Christian Education of Youth, Pope Pius XI emphasizes this duty in unmistakable terms. "There is no need," he writes, "to repeat what Our predecessors have declared on this point, especially Pius IX and Leo XIII . . . We renew and confirm their declarations, as well as the sacred Canons, in which the frequenting of non-Catholic schools, whether neutral or mixed, those namely which are open to Catholics and non-Catholics alike, is forbidden for Catholic children, and can be at most tolerated, on the approval of the Ordinary alone, under determined circumstances of place and time, and with special precautions.

"Neither can Catholics admit that other type of

mixed school . . . in which the students are provided with separate religious instruction, but receive
other lessons in common with non-Catholic pupils
from non-Catholic teachers. For the mere fact that
a school gives some religious instructions (often
extremely stinted) does not bring it into accord
with the rights of the Church and of the Christian
family, or make it a fit place for Catholic students.

Religion Must Pervade All Schools

"To be that, it is necessary that all the teaching
and the whole organization of the school, its teachers, syllabus, and textbooks in every branch, be
regulated by the Christian spirit, under the direc-
tion and maternal supervision of the Church; so
that religion may be in very truth the foundation
and crown of the youth's entire training; and this
in every grade of school, not only the elementary,
but the intermediate and the higher institutions of
learning as well. To use the words of Leo XIII:
'It is necessary not only that religious instruction
be given to the young at certain fixed times, but
also that every other subject taught be permeated
with Christian piety. If this is wanting, if this
sacred atmosphere does not pervade and warm the
hearts of masters and scholars alike, little good
can be expected from any kind of learning, and
considerable harm will often be the consequence.' "

Exceptional Cases

It is true, indeed, that Catholics who have had
the very best religious schooling and come from the

finest Catholic families sometimes fail nevertheless to turn out well; but that is certainly not because of, but despite, their religious education. Such cases, too, are relatively rare; and I think that on investigation it would be found that most of them were thrown too suddenly upon the world, or passed at too early an age beyond the sustaining and restraining influence of Christian surroundings. The great majority of men stand in need of the support and encouragement of a good example throughout their entire life; and as they cannot find this encouragement amid the hustle and bustle of the world, they must find it in their homes. It is not enough, then, that the child have the advantage of an early religious home training. The steadying influence of religion in the home must continue all through life.

The Grown-up Children

This phase of our subject, the necessity of religion in the home also for the children that have graduated from school and for the grown-up members of the family, ought perhaps to be emphasized most, because it is so commonly disregarded. It is with religion as with all other things that influence our lives: it must be fostered if its influence is to last; and once the child is beyond the school age, there is great danger that it will gradually limit its religious practice to the hour in church on Sundays, if a truly Christian home life does not continue the beneficial religious influence previously exerted by the Catholic school. The home is really the only place, besides the church, that can be made to conform to one's daily religious needs; and it is here, therefore, that one must provide what cannot be had abroad. If abroad, amid the enforced companionship of unbelieving fellow-workmen, it is not always possible to avoid hearing one's religion set at naught and ridiculed, in the home one can insist that it be held in honor and esteemed the most vital thing on earth. If abroad the open practice of any act of religion would ordinarily be viewed with silent wonder or unconcealed contempt, in the home the act of folding the hands or kneeling to pray must be regarded as natural as eating and drinking. If abroad one is often powerless to prevent irreligion and immorality from having access to the press, bill-boards, art galleries and places of amusement, one can at least refuse admission to them when they knock on the door of our Christian homes.

Give me truly Christian homes, homes in which Christianity is not merely tolerated but revered and fostered, and homes that *are* homes and not only sleeping quarters, and I will give you a race of Christian men and women who will cling to their Faith despite the insidious machinations of a corrupt and irreligious world.

III

Religion Prevents Divorce

It remains yet to touch briefly on a third reason why religion is indispensable in the home; the fact, namely, that without religion in the home the very existence of the family is in danger; for religion is the only sure safeguard of the indissolubility of marriage, the only bulwark against the breaking up of the family by divorce.

Where there is no religion, no supernatural motive to sustain and comfort them and no belief in the inviolability of the marriage vow, it is but natural that when difficulties that demand mutual forbearance arise, as they inevitably will, the husband or wife will have recourse to divorce. God Himself knows that it is by no means always an easy matter for husband and wife to bear with each other's shortcomings; that unaided human nature cannot perseveringly fulfill all the duties of wedded life; and for that very reason He supernaturalized Christian marriage, making it a sacrament that confers all the special graces needed to enable the married pair to perform their duties faithfully until death. It is mainly owing to the denial of the sacramental character of Matrimony, that marriage is entered into so lightly outside the Catholic Church, and that so little is made of the wide-spread evil of severing the marital union.

While we may rejoice that divorce is not prevalent among Catholics, we must nevertheless admit to our shame that divorced Catholics are not altogether unknown, and that not infrequently the strained relations between husband and wife and the breakdown of parental authority fall little short of the evils of actual divorce. It is not enough, therefore, that the religious character and the indissolubility of the matrimonial union be acknowledged. Religion must sanctify not only the beginning but the entire course of wedded and family life.

*   *   *   *

What a world of difference it would make in our lives, if among the requisites for an ideal home, the first place were assigned to religion! We say, "What is home without a mother?" and it is true that the absence of a good mother makes a gap that cannot be adequately filled. Yet how far, how unspeakably far, short of the ideal mother does she fall who does not foster religion in the home!

Religion a Gracious Queen

Why then are there so many homes, even Christian homes, where religion is notably lacking? Is it perhaps because religion is regarded as a tyrant ruling with an iron hand? Undoubtedly this view is responsible for the attitude of many who style themselves Christians. But no view could be farther from the truth. A real tyrant in the home, a tyrant whom many serve with slavish care, is the insatiable desire for ease, pleasure, or social standing, which forces families to live beyond their means in order to equal their neighbors in sumptuousness of board and luxury of equipment; while religion, whose sway would be that of a tender mother and gentle queen, is shown scant courtesy or even barred admission.

Welcome religion to your homes, therefore, fathers and mothers, sons and daughters, all ye who would be the possessors of truly happy homes. Welcome religion with open arms and gladsome hearts. Grossly do they err who look upon her as a tyrant. Religion is a queen, a most gracious queen, whose sway is as gentle as it is salutary. Yield yourselves to her loving influence so that the smile of her approval will ever beam upon you. Let her rule your going out and your coming in! Let her occupy the place of honor at your table! Let her sit with you in your study! Let her kindly eye restrain you in time of joy! Let her tender hand wipe away your tears in time of sorrow! Let her minister to you in time of illness and distress! Then, having received your last breath, she will conduct you at the last from the threshold of your earthly home to the eternal home of your Heavenly Father.

WHAT A GREAT ENEMY OF THE CHURCH SAID ABOUT THE FAMILY

Before his conversion, a great infidel made the following admission to the eminent apostle of the Sacred Heart, Father Mateo Crawley-Boevey, SS.CC.:—"We have only one object in view—to dechristianize the family. We are willing to let Catholics have their churches and chapels and cathedrals. We are satisfied to have the family. If we gain the family, our victory over the Church is assured."

CHAPTER II

Prayer in the Home

Irreligious Atmosphere

IN our day, irreligion may be said to pervade the very air we breathe. Just as our lungs inhale the germs of disease, and our bodies are coated with minute particles of dust, whenever we go abroad in a crowded city, so our souls, our memory and imagination, are exposed to an atmosphere tainted with irreligion whenever we go abroad into the world. To counteract the evil effects of a day's exposure to the smoke and dust of the city, we wash the stains from our bodies when we return home; we restore our lost vitality by partaking of wholesome food; and we fill our lungs with air free from the impurities that vitiate the atmosphere in factories and the busy marts of trade.

We must pursue a like course if we wish to render our souls immune from the contagion of irreligion. We must cleanse our souls from the dust of earthy and irreligious impressions that we acquire from contact with the wicked world. We must move about in a pure atmosphere from which all taint of irreligion is excluded. We must strengthen the Faith within us by nourishing our souls with wholesome mental food. To drop the metaphor, we must offset the irreligion that we daily encounter abroad, by prayer, by a Catholic atmosphere, and by good reading in the home.

32

I

Daily Prayer

The simplest, the easiest, the most ordinary, and still, for the individual, the most important exercise of the virtue of religion is prayer. Hence, if religion is to occupy that place in the home which we have seen it deserves, the members of the family must be faithful to the time-honored custom of daily prayer. No matter how old-fashioned and childish it may seem to some to insist on morning and evening prayer, grace before and after meals, and family prayers at certain seasons, it is these very things that establish religion firmly in the home, bring down Heaven's blessing, and give the home its true consecration. Show me a family where all the members are regular in saying their daily prayers, and I will show you a home where religion flourishes and peace and contentment reign. Show me a home where prayer is habitually neglected, and I will show you a family whose religion, if any still exist, is merely a matter of form.

Natural Place for Prayer

How, indeed, could it be otherwise? We have the duty of saving our immortal souls not only at the moment of death but all through life; and that duty necessarily implies keeping ourselves in the state of sanctifying grace. No one will remain long in the state of grace, if he is careless about his daily prayers; and few will pray daily, if they do not pray at home, because the home is the most convenient as it is the most natural place for one's regular daily prayer. What could be more natural for a man who believes that God is his Creator and Sovereign Lord, his greatest benefactor and best friend; who believes that we are in this world solely to do God's holy will and thus merit an eternal reward; what could be more natural, I ask, than for such a one to remember and to acknowledge this fact the first thing on awaking in the morning; to turn his first thoughts to God by blessing himself and making the good intention, and then to kneel down to pay his homage to his Creator, to thank Him for His endless favors, to renew his fealty to Him, and to implore His blessing? And what more natural as well as more wise and fitting than for him to do the like in the evening before he commits himself to the night's sleep from which he never knows whether he will awaken?

It is not necessary to devote a great deal of time to one's morning and evening prayer. For the ordinary layman five minutes will usually suffice; and, if necessary, one can say a really devout morning or evening prayer, embracing all the essentials, in two or three minutes. The important thing is to be regular about it; to have a regular formula or number of prayers to say; to say them at a regular time, and in a certain regular manner. If you like to use a book, you will do well to do so. The use of a book helps to fix the habit of praying. But such is in nowise necessary. Only have some definite prayers to say as the minimum and say that minimum well.

How Much Must One Pray?

But what should be the minimum for a good morning or evening prayer? That depends on various circumstances—one's age, one's leisure, one's needs, and also on the extent to which one makes use of the other means of grace—the Mass and Holy Communion. It is plain that not all have the time for the same amount of prayer in the morning. Some find it more convenient to say only a short prayer in the morning but a long prayer at night. Others are accustomed to say the greater part of their prayers in church during the day. A certain doctor of my acquaintance has the very praise-worthy habit of praying for about a quarter of an hour in church on his way home every evening. Nor do all need the same amount of prayer. Persons exposed to greater temptations, or subject to evil habits, as well as persons bound to a more perfect life must pray more than persons not thus circumstanced. But all must pray enough to enable them to live habitually in the state of sanctifying grace. So much is certain: if one falls into mortal sin, the reason is to be sought in the insufficiency of one's prayers or in the infrequency of one's reception of the sacraments. While it is impossible, therefore, to determine just what prayers each one should say in the morning or in the evening or even each day, it seems to me that our daily prayers should always include the acts of Faith, Hope, Charity, contrition and thanksgiving, the Apostles' Creed, and several Our Fathers and Hail Marys.

Pray on Your Knees!

In regard to the manner of praying, it is best to say your morning prayer after you are dressed; your evening prayer before undressing, and both *on your knees.* This last point is of great importance. In the first place, the act of kneeling is itself equivalent to a prayer, being an act of adoration, and it is unquestionably the most becoming posture in which to address ourselves to our Creator. Then the practice of kneeling to say our prayers has the good effect of reminding us of that duty. If we want to say our prayers only while dressing or undressing or when in bed, the chances are that in many cases they will be said poorly or be altogether forgotten. And lastly, the habit of kneeling at our morning and evening prayers will have a most edifying effect on others in the household. Even though each one prays in the privacy of his room, it will be generally known in the family that one is accustomed to pray on bended knees, and that knowledge will be of inestimable value in mutually encouraging one another never to abandon the practice. When brothers occupy the same room, or sisters share the same apartment, the practice is of still greater importance for their mutual edification. Yet most important of all is that parents who are still able to kneel, do so and thus give a good example to their children.

The Parents' Example

Setting a good example in this matter of prayer

is a part of the religious education which parents owe to their children. And what a beneficial influence it will have upon the children all through life, if the parents not only teach them from their tenderest years to pray but also pray with them; and even when they are grown up, let them always be aware of the fact that their parents, too, prostrate themselves morning and evening on their knees in order to pay homage to their God. Nothing will impress more deeply on the child that prayer is not merely a child's duty but a duty for life; that religion is something not only for the church but for the home as well; that there is nothing about praying or kneeling for anyone to be ashamed of; but rather that it would be a cause of shame for any Christian, be he old or young, to be obliged to admit that he did not daily lift his hands and his heart to God in prayer.

How well do I remember the splendid example that my own father gave in this respect. Every evening without fail he would kneel, entirely free of any support, before a Crucifix in the living room, and with devoutly folded hands, and body as upright as a mountain pine perform his evening devotions.

II

Grace at Meals

But it is not enough that each and every member of the family have the habit of saying his morning and evening prayers. Where religion flourishes in the home as it should, if the family is truly to deserve the name Christian, there must be found also the age-old Christian custom of saying grace before and after meals. This venerable custom is the inevitable consequence of a Christian outlook on life. If we believe that God is the author and sustainer of life, that "every best gift and every perfect gift is from above, coming down from the Father of lights" (Jas. 1, 17) then surely we should be mindful of our indebtedness to our Heavenly Father at least as often as we partake of the food by which our mortal life is sustained. Our blessed Savior expressly teaches us to pray: "Give us this day our daily bread"; and what time could be more fitting for the fulfillment of that duty than the hour of our daily meals?

A Profession of Faith

There is, however, yet another important aspect to the practice of saying grace in the home. To pray in the presence of others is a profession of one's Faith; and for that reason alone, if for no other, the practice should be fostered. You simply cannot make your religion a strictly interior affair, just as little as you can make it exclusively a church affair. If you sow good seed in a fertile soil and take care that it receives the necessary warmth and moisture, the seed will not long remain hidden but will sprout forth and give unmistakable evidence of the living principle within. It is exactly the same with religion. The man that really has deep religious convictions will also show them exteriorly at the opportune time and place. Only those Christians whose Faith is not deeply rooted or who have been

misled by the unchristian fashion of the day will
say: "I believe in praying without attracting notice.
There is no use making a show every time a person
wants to pray." Indeed not; and it is to be presumed that thousands of Catholics pray frequently,
even in company, without others being aware of it.
I am willing, too, to pardon them if they offer that
excuse for not praying openly in public eating
houses, but not when there is a question of meal
prayers in the privacy of one's own home.

But someone might say: "I don't see the value
of such a profession of Faith in the home. Everyone at home knows my religious convictions; so why
need I manifest them by blessing myself or saying
grace at table?" One might argue with just as much
logic: "I don't see the need of showing the members
of my family that I love them. They know that I
love them, and that love is an affair of the heart.
So why should I give token of my love by my looks,
manner, words, or actions?" Just as the person who
shows little love for the members of his household
really has little love for them; so he, too, who cares
not to manifest his religion to them very likely has
precious little religion left in his heart. Interior
virtues must needs be exercised by exterior acts;
otherwise, they will wither away and finally perish
altogether.

Prayer Necessary for Salvation

It is quite true that there is no positive law com-
manding us to pray before and after meals. Neither
is there such a law requiring us to say our morning

and evening prayers. But nothing is more certain than that we are obliged to pray, and that, for adults, prayer is an indispensable means of salvation. And since a more fitting time for prayer can scarcely be found than the hour of rising, the hour of retiring, and the meal hours, it is much to be feared that those who do not pray at these times do not pray at all, or at least not enough to satisfy the obligation of prayer. It will doubtless be found that usually those that are most conscientious about saying these customary prayers are also the ones that pray most at other times and make the most frequent use of the Mass and the sacraments.

Let me beg the reader, therefore, not to dismiss the question of saying grace as a trifling matter. A drop of rain is also a small matter; yet every rain, the heaviest as well as the lightest, is made up of drops. In particular as a means of making religion flourish in the home, the value of prayer at meals can hardly be overestimated. To say grace before and after every meal means to worship God, to profess your Faith, and to edify your neighbor six times a day, 180 times a month, and more than two thousand times a year. Small as the single prayers may be, and insignificant as may seem their effect, the total sum will amount to a great deal and is sure to bring down a shower of blessings.

III

Family Prayer

"Where there are two or three gathered together in my name, there am I in the midst of them" (Mt. 18,

20). By these words our blessed Savior clearly ascribes a special power and a special blessing to prayers said jointly with others; and we may be sure that if this is true of any group of persons gathered together in His name, it is doubly true of the Christian family, which is knit together not only by the strongest ties of mutual love but also by the consecration of a sacrament. All the good effects that flow from prayers said by the individual, will accrue in still greater abundance from family prayer. In their pastoral letter to all American Catholics some years ago (1920) our Bishops expressed themselves on this point as follows: "We heartily commend the beautiful practice of family prayer. . . . The presence of Jesus will surely be a source of blessing to the home where parents and children unite to offer up prayer in common. The spirit of piety which this custom develops will sanctify the bonds of family love and ward off the dangers which often bring sorrow and shame. We appeal in this matter with special earnestness to young fathers and mothers, who have it in their power to mould the hearts of their children and train them betimes in the habit of prayer."

Example of Tobias

It is to young parents, too, nay, to newly married couples, that I would appeal not to await the appearance of children, but to begin to pray in common from the very outset of their wedded life. While everything is new and family traditions are only in the making, it will be an easy matter for them to

establish the custom of family prayer; whereas early
neglect may allow a contrary custom to get so firmly
rooted that it will be hard to break. Would that all
newly married couples would follow the beautiful
example of the younger Tobias and his wife Sara.
"We are the children of saints," he said, "and must
not be joined together like heathens that know not
God" (Tob. 8, 5). Accordingly they did not wait
until the wedding festivities and their honeymoon
were over before thinking of praying in common
but the very first night after their marriage "prayed
earnestly, both together, that health might be given
them" and that God would bless their union.

Family Worship a Duty

To anyone that gives the matter serious thought
the neglect of family prayer in a Christian family
must seem well-nigh impossible. It is to be supposed, namely, that the head of a Christian family
esteems the Faith as his greatest treasure, as worth
more to himself and to every member of his household than any amount of earthly goods. It is further to be presumed that, valuing his faith as he
does, he will be most solicitous about preserving it
so as to insure its blessings for himself and his
family. On such a supposition, is it possible that
he will relegate all prayer to the privacy of each
one's room and never have the family pray aloud
in common? Just as little as he would have each
member of the family take his meals alone and
never do any work or have any recreation in common. As long as the family circle, family meals,

family picnics remain in the families of civilized communities, so long will also family prayer be fostered in every truly Christian home. For, even apart from the value of family prayer as a means of securing the blessings of religion, it will ever be incumbent on the family as a specific duty. The family is a perfect natural society, a distinct entity in itself; and as such it owes God an act of common worship. It is not enough that the single members of the family practice their religion; the family itself *as a society* must pay its homage to the Creator and Lord of the family; and this is done by family prayer.

Saying Grace Aloud

How often this duty will be performed, will depend on each family's devotion, and more particularly on the religious zeal of the parents. In families where different members rise at different hours, it is usually unpractical, if not impossible, to recite the morning prayer in common; but the evening prayer could easily be a family prayer, especially in young families; and this practice is most heartily to be recommended. There is no valid excuse anywhere, however, for not saying grace at meals aloud together; and I hope that no father or mother who reads this will fail to introduce the practice, if it does not yet exist in their families. The prayer most suited for this purpose is without doubt the "Our Father," to which may be appropriately added the "Hail Mary" and, before meals, "Bless us, O Lord, etc." and after meals, "We thank Thee, O

Lord, etc." To recite these three prayers aloud, slowly and distinctly, and to make the sign of the cross before and after, requires no more than one minute of time. Surely no Christian can be so niggardly with God as to say that that is too much; or to contend that to devote a minute to prayer before and after each meal would be to convert the home into a monastery. Yet I pronounce no anathema against the family that is content with less. Where appetites are especially keen, the chances are that the saying of a short prayer is more likely to become regular than the saying of a long one. And hence, as a compromise, I would suggest that the afore-mentioned prayers be said in common at least before and after the principal meal, and that a part of them be said at the other meals.

Seasonal Devotions

In addition to daily family prayers, there should be also seasonal prayers in common in all Christian families, especially during the months of May and October and during the holy seasons of Advent and Lent. There are, it is true, special devotions in church at these seasons, two or three times a week; but a good Catholic should not be content with these. If the family is to share the blessings of religion to the full, the changes of the ecclesiastical year, which are so striking a feature of the services in church, should be reflected also in the home. Very suitable for these seasonal devotions in the home are the approved litanies of the Sacred Heart, the Holy Name, the Blessed Virgin, and St. Joseph, and above all the rosary. The rosary, with its joyful, sorrowful, and glorious mysteries, is appropriate for every season; is made up of the best of all prayers; can be lengthened or shortened according to pleasure; is easily recited by even a small child, and is enriched with numerous indulgences. Consisting, too, as it does of a number of different prayers linked together by the consideration of a certain mystery for the purpose of praising God, the rosary is a fitting symbol of the Christian family, whose members are united by the bonds of blood and religion; who share joys, sorrows, and glories in common; and who work together for a common end— their temporal and eternal welfare and happiness.

Overcoming Bashfulness

I realize that in families where the custom does not exist, a certain bashfulness in regard to spiritual matters will have to be overcome in order to make a start; but once the ice is broken and a beginning made, it will be easy to develop the practice. Women and girls are usually less backward than men and boys in these matters; and as in so many other worthy causes, so here, too, let them take the initiative. They know how to coax the men folk in order to attain their own personal aims. Let them employ the same knowledge for the benefit of the entire family. God will most certainly reward them richly if they establish in the family this pious practice of saying the rosary; for to them will go the credit of enriching their home with those spiritual roses that fill it with the fragrance of Heaven's blessing.

The Golden Mean

It is hardly necessary to remind parents that even in fostering so praiseworthy a practice as family prayer, they should not attempt too much. As in all things, so here, too, one must observe the golden mean. Children cannot be expected to devote as much time to prayer as their elders do, or should do. They naturally take more to play than to prayer; and if they are indiscreetly obliged to take part in interminable prayers, there is danger of creating in them a distaste for prayer. Such a method defeats its own end. The object in accustoming children to say their prayers regularly from the time they begin to talk, is to develop in them a love of prayer and a realization of the need of it. This can be done while their hearts are still pliable by teaching them very short prayers as early as possible, and by gradually making them understand that when they pray they are speaking to the good God, from whom all blessings flow; to their loving Jesus, who came upon earth that they might come to Heaven; and to the Mother of Jesus or to their Guardian Angel and the Saints.

Making Prayer Spontaneous

This background of religious truth and Gospel story is of the greatest importance in teaching the young to love prayer and to feel the need of it; and it should not be hard for any mother who has a little piety herself to instill into her children such an appreciation of God's greatness, goodness and power that prayer will come natural to them as the spontaneous utterance of their grateful and confiding hearts. Or would it really be so hard, even before the infants are able to speak, to make the sign of the cross over them and to say a brief morning and evening prayer aloud in their stead, thus accustoming them to the sound of the words, so that "the good God" or "Jesus" or "Mary" might be the first word their innocent lips would utter?

Would it not be easy to show them pictures of Jesus and tell them stories of Jesus, as their understanding develops—stories of His childhood, of Bethlehem, the stable, Mary and Joseph, the singing angels and the adoring shepherds—stories of His public life—how He loved children, how the crowds followed Him, how He went about doing good? Remember, mothers, that your little ones' sanctified souls are hungry for knowledge of God and holy things. So tell them how much God loves them; that it is God who made all the good and beautiful things they see—the fruits and flowers, the trees and bushes and grass, the birds and the fishes, the soft-furred kitten and the friendly dog. Tell them, too, how poor Jesus was; that He became poor for love of us. Speak to them of Jesus in the Tabernacle, and awaken in them a desire to visit Him. In this way, not by threatening or scolding but by gently leading and by instilling knowledge which will of itself yield motives for prayer, you will surely implant deep in them for life, if not a love, at least a strong feeling of the appropriateness of daily prayer.

Mothers of Future Saints

But to pursue such a course, some may say, would be to try to make a saint out of every child. Well, is that such an awful possibility to contemplate? Somewhere in the world to-day are the mothers of the saints of to-morrow; and not of the saints only but of the criminals also; of the great as well as the lowly, the heroes and the outcasts, the successes and the failures. You know not what latent possibilities are in your child. Of one thing only are you sure, that one day he will be numbered either among the elect or the reprobate. What his eternal lot will be, will depend largely upon his practice or his neglect of prayer. Have a care, mother dear, lest his neglect of it be laid to your charge.

Jacob's Ladder

When Jacob, the son of Isaac, fled from the anger of his brother, Esau, into the land of Haran, he pursued his journey until after sunset; and then, weary and footsore, he laid himself down to sleep, resting his head on a stone. While he slept God appeared to him in a wondrous vision. He saw a ladder that reached from earth to Heaven, and on it angels of God ascending and descending. And the Lord himself, leaning on the top of the ladder, spoke to him saying: "I am the Lord God of Abraham thy father, and the God of Isaac . . . In thee and thy seed, all the tribes of the earth shall be blessed. And I will be thy keeper whithersoever thou goest, and will bring thee back into this land: neither will

I leave thee, till I shall have accomplished all that I have said."

Upon awaking, Jacob trembled and exclaimed full of awe: "Indeed, the Lord is in this place . . . This is no other than the house of God and the gate of Heaven" (Gen. 29).

The ladder which Jacob beheld in his dream, with angels ascending and descending, is an appropriate symbol of the prayers that ascend to Heaven from the Christian home and bring down God's blessing on its inmates. Would to God that such a ladder would rise to Heaven from the home of every family in the land! If you would have God's angels bear His special blessing to your homes, Christian parents; if you wish the Lord to be your keeper and to abide in your home; if you would be led back to your true home, the land of your Heavenly Father;—then let your prayers ascend to Heaven like a cloud of precious incense morning, noon, and night, and God will look down upon your home with special favor. In very truth may it then be said of your home what Jacob said of the place of his vision: "Indeed, the Lord is in this place." During life it will be a house of God, and at the end of life the gate to Heaven.

CHAPTER III

Catholic Atmosphere in the Home

"In order to obtain perfect education, it is of the utmost importance to see that all those conditions which surround the child during the period of his formation, in other words, the combination of circumstances which we call environment, correspond exactly to the end proposed. The first natural and necessary element in this environment, as regards education, is the family, and this precisely because so ordained by the Creator Himself."

—Pius XI in "Christian Education of Youth."

Need of Healthy Atmosphere

TO enjoy the great boon of good health, it is not enough for one to be cleanly in one's person, to partake of sufficient wholesome food and drink, and to take a proper amount of exercise. Many a child in the crowded districts of our great centers of industry has plenty of good food and exercise and has been taught by a loving mother to cultivate the habit of personal cleanliness, and yet is far from enjoying good health. Living in the shadow of huge buildings, breathing in constantly the smoke and dust of near-by factories that becloud and bedim the small portion of sunlight that it receives, instead of attaining the full vigor and sprightliness of the normal child, it must languish and pale like a flower in a sterile soil. But take this child from these unpropitious surroundings; place it in the country far from the dusty city; let it bask in a glory of sunshine and drink deep draughts of pure country air; and the bloom that will redden its cheeks, the sparkle that will light up its eyes, and the lilt that will appear in its gait will proclaim the beneficial effects of such a change. The one thing that was wanting to the child was a healthy atmosphere; and such an atmosphere we must all have in order to remain in a state of perfect health.

Now what is true of the body and natural life is equally true of the soul and the religious life. If the vitality of a Catholic's Faith is not to be gradually weakened by the contagion of irreligion that infests practically our entire public life, he must be able to spend the greater part of his private life in a place where the moral atmosphere is not only not tainted but is positively religious; and this he will be able to do only if he have a morally healthy and religiously bracing atmosphere in his own home.

Atmosphere of the Home

The reader will readily understand that in homes where family prayer is regularly practiced, much has already been done to create a religious atmosphere; for by the atmosphere of the home I mean, broadly speaking, the aggregate of external influences in the home, affecting the spirituality of the members of the family; and, in a narrower sense, the sum-total of sensible objects in the home capable of exerting a favorable or unfavorable influence upon the religious or moral life of its inmates. Just as we are variously affected as regards our bodies by the material atmosphere in which we live,—by its heat and cold, by the gases and germs and minute particles of dust that it holds: so, too, are our souls affected by the sensible objects around us; and the aggregate of such objects is accordingly quite appropriately called moral atmosphere.

Effect of Environment

That the moral atmosphere or environment, as it may also be styled, exerts a strong influence upon a man's habits and the formation of his character, no one that has the slightest knowledge of human nature will presume to deny. It is a principle of sound philosophy that there is no conception in the mind which is not preceded by a perception of one of the five senses; and since it is the mind and will that govern our rational actions, it follows that our sense-perceptions, notably those of seeing and hearing, must have a powerful influence upon our actions. Absolutely speaking, of course, a person may shake off this influence; but the important thing to be noted is that the influence is there and is felt even though it be withstood; and since we must be guided by what ordinarily happens and not by what is theoretically possible, parents and other responsible persons should see to it that the moral atmosphere in their home is such as will exert a wholesome influence on all in the household. It is true, the influence exerted by environment produces its effects slowly and perhaps imperceptibly; but it may not for that reason be belittled or ignored, any more than the slowly but constantly dripping water which little by little hollows the stone.

I

A Worldly Atmosphere

To state in the first place what the moral atmosphere of the home should not be, if it is to meet the requirements of a truly Christian home, I would say that it should not be worldly. Worldliness is diametrically opposed to religion. The spirit of the Catholic religion is the spirit of the Gospel, and the name for that spirit is unworldliness. The whole purpose of the Catholic religion is to turn our thoughts, our hopes, our aspirations and our efforts away from this world to the other world; and we are good Catholics only in so far as we realize this end. Christ tells us plainly: "You cannot serve two masters." We cannot serve God and the world. Yet one of the two we must serve. Hence we are obliged to choose either the one or the other. If we choose to serve God, if we want to rule our life according to the precepts of the Gospel, then we must banish worldliness from our homes. If we fail to banish worldliness even from our homes, which we are free to fashion to suit our own tastes and to meet our own wants, then we plainly show that the world still has a place in our hearts.

Extravagant Furnishings

But how does this worldliness manifest itself in the home? When may the atmosphere of the home be said to have a worldly character? First of all, when its dominant note is luxury or extravagance.

If the Christian's attitude towards wealth must square with those two statements of Our Lord: "Blessed are the poor in spirit," and "How hardly shall they that have riches enter into the Kingdom of God" (Mk., 10, 23), then it is plainly an evidence of worldliness, or opposition to the spirit of Christianity, if wealth obtrudes itself in the home from every nook and corner. I do not say that a rich Catholic may not have a splendid home, furnished in a manner suited to his station in life. But there should be no boldly conspicuous display of wealth, evidencing an inordinate love of worldly magnificence and a disposition to glory in it. That would show a worldly spirit.

But it is not only the rich who may sin by extravagance. Families of the middle class are just as often guilty. The homes of such families betray a very decided spirit of worldliness when they are quite evidently furnished more richly than the owners' modest means can afford. We are in conscience bound to make a discreet use of our earthly goods and to make our expenditures in proportion to our means. The endeavor to match the splendor of one's own home with that of the homes of one's more well-to-do acquaintances proceeds from pride and leads to other unchristian practices besides the misapplication of one's earthly goods. In order to be able to earn more money to spend on luxuries, some young wives persist in retaining the gainful positions which they had before marriage, and for the sake of this filthy lucre sinfully postpone the task of rearing a family. That is the worst kind of worldliness—the kind that weighs duty and worldly goods in the balance and deliberately chooses the latter. Beware of it, my dear young couples! Beware!*

Extravagance in Dress

What has been said of excessive expenditures for the furnishing and decorating of one's home, is equally true of extravagance in ornamenting one's person. The home may be given a worldly touch by the unduly rich or extremely stylish apparel of the persons that dwell in it. One is certainly allowed to dress well and becomingly within the limits of one's means and according to the requirements of one's station in life; but in no station in life is there an excuse for extravagance. There may be no injustice to anyone if a woman buys all the exquisite gowns, rare jewels, and costly footwear and headgear that she can possibly pay for; but neither is there any charity in it or Christian moderation; and justice is not the only virtue that must regulate the use we make of our worldly goods. We are bound also by the law of moderation and of charity; and it is sinful to waste money for the extravagant decoration of one's person or one's home when there are thousands of deserving poor who have not even the necessary food, clothing, and shelter.

Keeping a Family Budget

The best way for parents to avoid excessive or ill-advised expenditures is to keep a family budget. Let them make a careful study of their resources

*See quotation on following page.

Pope Pius XI on Mothers Who Work Away from Home

"Mothers will above all devote their work to the home and the things connected with it. Intolerable and to be opposed with all our strength is the abuse whereby mothers of families, because of the insufficiency of the father's salary, are forced to engage in gainful occupations outside the domestic walls, to the neglect of their own proper cares and duties, particularly the education of their children."

—Encyclical "Quadragesimo Anno," on the Social Order.

N. B.—If His Holiness condemns the abuse whereby mothers are forced to work away from their homes, what must he think of those mothers, who, without any compulsion whatever, entirely of their own accord, pursue gainful occupations outside the domestic walls?

and a classified list of their needs; e.g., housing, food, clothing, running expenses, improvement, and savings. Then let them fix a certain percentage of their income for each of these items of expense, and hold their disbursements strictly within the budget allowance, unless real necessity or charity require otherwise. It is hardly necessary to remark that also such expenses as church, school and club dues, charity and amusements must be figured in the budget, and that according to the aforesaid classification these, together with all outlays for reading material, could be put under the heading improvement; that is, mental, moral, or physical. Keeping a home and family is just as much a business as running a store; so why should it not be kept on a business basis? Many couples have had their eyes opened by keeping an itemized account of disbursements. They found that they had been extravagant without realizing it. But if keeping tab on one's expenses teaches economy, it should be done in every Christian home; for economy, supernaturalized, is nothing but the Christian virtue of moderation.

A Touch of Paganism

Another indication of worldliness in the home is the unchristian and sometimes even pagan character of the objects with which it is equipped. Let us enter such a home. What do we see? At our very entrance, perhaps, a painting of Apollo dancing with thin-clad muses on the lawn; there a lamp or candlelabrum supported by the nude figure of

Cupid; in a corner, perhaps, a statue of Venus of Milo; on the library table various gay-colored magazines displaying bathing girls or notorious "movie" actresses on the front covers; on the mantle a snow-white bust of Pallas or some other mythological deity; and here and there as we wander through the various apartments, sundry other ornaments and articles of a like character. Will any Catholic maintain that such objects are appropriate in a Christian home? Yet there are Catholic homes, and not a few of them, in which such ornaments are quite common. In some cases their presence is due to mere thoughtlessness or sheer worldly-mindedness, and no conscience is made of it. In others, however, a sense of guilt is manifested by the care with which such objects are removed when a visit of the pastor or some other clergyman is expected.

Regard for Modesty

To be in thorough accord with its profession of Christianity, the home of a Catholic family should be free from all things of this kind. The home is not an art museum; and statues of pagan deities that may be tolerated in museums are out of place in a Christian home. And so, too, are all images not in conformity with Christian modesty. It will not be enough to limit them to a small representation. Neither will it suffice to confine them to one place, say the reception room, in order that there at least you may show your broadmindedness to the non-Catholics who enter your home. No; a Catholic home should contain nothing that proclaims sympathy with the spirit of the world. One picture, one statue, one ornament may mar the character of an entire room and thwart the good effect that other images are calculated to produce. Away, then, Catholic fathers and mothers, with all worldliness from your homes! You are exposed enough to its contagion when you go abroad. At least be quit of it when you enter the sanctuary of your own home.

An Insidious Propaganda

If pictures and statues of persons insufficiently clad give an air of worldliness to the home, what must be the effect of such lack of modesty in the living inmates? There is an insidious propaganda abroad in our day to tear down the conventions that Christian civilization has established as safeguards of the virtue of purity. Despite the specious reasons advanced in its defense; e.g., that one should become familiar with the nude in order not to be affected by it, the plain purpose of this propaganda is to substitute a pagan code for our Christian code of morality. This purpose is the more evident since some of the more outspoken adherents of the movement have declared that the Ten Commandments are antiquated and that there is no longer such a thing as sin. In view of this threat of paganism, the duty of Catholics is clear. Neither in the home nor elsewhere may there be any letting down of the bars of decency and Christian propriety. And mothers should so train their children from childhood on that they will never presume to appear in the presence of others without being modestly covered.

Those girls who make no conscience of exposing themselves in the presence of their sisters, will gradually come to make nothing of wearing insufficient clothing in public. And when modesty is thrown to the winds, purity will not be slow to follow.

II

A Catholic Atmosphere

Worldliness, then, must be banished from the Christian home, if the latter is to fulfill its mission of helping the individual Catholic to resist the enticements of the world. Yet when we have purified our homes of worldliness, our task is not yet completed. We must provide also a distinctly Catholic atmosphere. There are Catholic homes, or I should say rather, there are homes of Catholics, that do not contain the slightest evidence of the religion of those that dwell in them. You may see there pictures of beautiful birds and horses and dogs; of landscapes and castles; of distinguished authors, musicians and statesmen; but you will look in vain for any religious token of a distinctly Catholic character. The occupants of such homes justify this want by saying that they do not believe in parading their religion before the world. I agree that ordinarily we need not parade our religion before the world; but are we doing that when we give it scope within the sacred precincts of our own homes? The Catholic who fails to avail himself of the external aids to religion provided by religious objects in the home shows that religion is not a dominant factor in his life.

Portraits of Your Friends

By all means, therefore, let there be some distinctly Catholic images in your home, if you wish to enjoy the advantages of a healthy Catholic atmosphere. Far from being singular or obtrusive, nothing could be more natural or more appropriate. If you hang portraits of your relatives and friends and of eminent men and women on the walls of your home, should you not do as much for the best of all your friends and the greatest of all illustrious men and women—Our Blessed Lord and the saints? There is no valid reason why these latter should be restricted to the bedrooms or to some obscure corners. It is true, the home is not a church; and if one has a special place at home for prayer, a little shrine to which one can withdraw for undisturbed communion with God, it is quite proper that it be in a somewhat secluded spot. Neither is the home a church goods store; and it may be no impiety, therefore, if some one expresses his dislike of a home so crowded with religious pictures that they seem to be on display for sale. Allowance must be made in this matter for individual tastes. Some delight in a profusion of ornamentation, while others are for using it very sparingly. But whether your taste favors much or little decoration in the home, see to it that the religious element is not stinted.

The Chief Symbol of Your Faith

Foremost among the religious articles that should have a place of honor in every Catholic home is the Crucifix, the image of our crucified Savior. The

Cross is the principal emblem of the Catholic religion; it is the symbol of our Faith, the source of our hope, the incentive to our love, the sign of our redemption, the pledge of our salvation. A beautiful and also moderately large Crucifix should be one of the finest and most cherished ornaments in the home. But there should be at least a small yet properly fashioned Crucifix also in each one of the bedrooms. It is deplorable that so many Catholics are satisfied with any kind of Crucifix, no matter how poorly it is made. They can afford to have large and expensive portraits of their parents and children, but balk at spending a few dollars for a worthy image of their crucified Savior. Let them remember that just as their taste is betrayed by the other objects, so the depth of their Faith is indicated by the quality of the religious images with which their home is equipped.

Image of the Sacred Heart

Other images that should be seen in every Catholic home are a picture of the Holy Family and of the Sacred Heart of Jesus. Pope Leo XIII prescribed that all Christian families should be consecrated to the Holy Family; and Our Lord revealed to St. Margaret Mary that He would bless all houses where an image of His Sacred Heart would be exposed and honored. The choice of other pictures must be left to each one's individual taste and devotion, always, however, in entire accord with the teaching of our holy religion and the spirit of Holy Mother Church. A picture of the Child Jesus or of the Guardian Angel would be very appropriate for the children's apartments; and one of the Blessed Virgin and of St. Joseph in the rooms of the larger girls and boys respectively. In each bedroom, at least, there should be a vase with holy water, which should be religiously used on rising and before retiring. And in a becoming place, one should preserve some blessed palm branches and at least two blessed candles, the latter in suitable candlesticks.

Unedifying Pictures

While, as I have said, the selection of the different images must be left to each one's own taste, one quality must be insisted on as indispensable: the images must be such as will edify. If they are not of a nature to edify, then they cannot possibly produce the effect that they are employed to produce; namely, a wholesome Catholic atmosphere. The requirement that the pictures be edifying may seem to be rather vague and indefinite; but it furnishes a working rule that will answer all practical purposes. The main thing is to eliminate all images that are not edifying; and such one may call all those that represent Our Lord or the saints in a manner unworthy of them; that is to say, in an attitude or attire or in circumstances in which they themselves would certainly not wish to be pictured or seen. If no one would feel himself honored to find a caricature or other unworthy representation of himself on the wall of your home, how can you

expect by means of similar pictures to please Our
Lord and the saints?

Untrue to History

It is no excuse to say that a certain picture is true
to history, that it merely represents an actual fact
in the life of the saint. That an immoral pagan
judge subjected a saint to indignities does not justify us in repeating the indecency on canvas. But
many representations lack even this flimsy excuse,
as they are positively untrue to history. In the Gospel story of the birth of our Savior, for example,
we are told that the Virgin Mother wrapped the
Babe in swaddling clothes; yet we find pictures
inscribed "The Nativity" in which the Divine
Child is not only not wrapped in swaddling clothes
but not clad at all. The same is true of the Christ
Child on many Madonnas. No one will maintain
that such a representation is true to history.
Neither is it true to the highest standard of Catholic art; and least of all is it true to that reverent
delicacy of treatment due to the august person of
the Child Divine.

I realize quite well that strict insistence on this
rule will debar many a picture from the Catholic
home. Be it so. There are hundreds of other sacred
pictures to choose from,—pictures that are in every
way satisfactory, in point of art no less than in
point of propriety. Let such only adorn your walls,
and the sight of them will be to you a source not
only of edification in your daily life but of consolation and encouragement in days of sorrow and

distress; and a daily reminder that if you but imitate the example of the saints whom they represent, you too will one day share their happiness.

Good Example

In the foregoing pages, I have dwelt only on
the visible objects that give character to the home
—on what I have called its moral atmosphere in the
narrow sense. It will be remembered, however, that
I defined the home atmosphere also in a broader
sense; namely, as the aggregate of external influences in the home affecting the spiritual life of the
inmates. In this broader sense, the words and deeds
of the inmates also contribute essentially to the
moral atmosphere, and if the latter is to be thoroughly Catholic, the general tone of conversation
and conduct in the home must reflect a Catholic
mentality. The Holy Father emphasizes this point
in the following passage of His Encyclical on the
Christian Education of Youth: "That education,
as a rule, will be more effective and lasting which
is received in a well-ordered and well-disciplined
Christian family; and the more efficacious in proportion to the clear and constant good example set
first by the parents and then by the other members
of the household."

The Catholic Mind

One cannot, it is true, in view of human frailty,
expect that the members of even the better Catholic families will never be guilty of wrong-doing of
any kind. But what can be expected is that when

wrong-doing does occur, it will be found to be out of keeping with the surroundings. In other words, should deviations from Catholic standards sometimes occur in practice, there should at least be no deviation from Catholic principles in theory. Should the conversation, for example, turn on such subjects as Sunday observance, frequent Communion, mixed marriages, cremation, forbidden societies and books, attendance of Catholics at non-Catholic schools, the relations between Church and State and the like, the attitude of the Church will be accepted without question. The accepted stand of every member of the family will be the same as that of the Church; and if in any instance any member should mistakingly espouse a contrary opinion, he will at once recede from it when assured that it is not in accord with the teaching of Holy Mother Church. This is what is meant by the Latin phrase "sentire cum ecclesia," "to be of one mind with the Church," to have the Catholic mentality or the Catholic mind. In homes where such a mentality prevails nothing will be found that antagonizes the Church. No songs will be heard that offend against Christian virtue; no literature will be tolerated that openly or insidiously undermines Catholic morals; and no radio programs will be listened to that disseminate false doctrines of a religious or moral character.

Homes of the Early Christians

Would to God there were more Catholic homes of this kind scattered up and down our beloved land, homes that are in every sense Catholic and veritable strongholds of Christianity! Some will no doubt aver that it is an idle dream to expect an increase in the number of such homes amid the adverse conditions of our age. But are the conditions of our age any worse than were the conditions of pagan Rome? The moral atmosphere of Rome at the dawn of Christianity was so corrupt that vice was not only tolerated but even enthroned as a god in certain forms of religious worship. Yet, despite the universal corruption without, so pure, so holy and so heavenly an atmosphere pervaded the homes of the Christians that it not only kept their minds untainted and their hearts unsullied, but, by its own superior power expanding and radiating from those homes, gradually purified even the public atmosphere and in the end brought about the conversion of the entire Roman people.

Who shall say that what was accomplished in those days is impossible of accomplishment now? It would require perhaps a miracle of grace; but the days of miracles are not over. Catholic families, however, need not look so far ahead nor to such far reaching results for inducements to preserve a Catholic atmosphere in their homes. Such an atmosphere will offer them full and immediate compensation for the pains required to maintain it. It will keep their religion pure and undefiled and keep them unspotted of this world.

CHAPTER IV

Good Reading in the Home

Culture an Ally of Religion

BECAUSE of the great emphasis that the Church incessantly lays upon the supreme importance of the supernatural goods and objects of life, a Catholic might easily be led to the conclusion that all merely natural attainments are to be despised and neglected. Such a conclusion would be unwarranted, as was pointed out to the present writer himself, when, as a small boy, he protested that there was no use in learning grammar, because one 'didn't need to know grammar to get to Heaven.' While it is quite true that the possession of sanctifying grace and of the supernatural virtues is of such tremendous importance that all other things of earth pale into insignificance by comparison; while we must admit that a rude and unlettered but upright and religious man will fare better on the day of judgment than the educated but unprincipled villain who passes in the eyes of the world for a refined gentleman; while, in fine, it is undeniable that genuine virtue can exist without the conventional graces of society, and that faultless manners do not imply interior worth; yet it is none the less certain that culture of mind as well as urbanity of speech are powerful allies of religion; that virtue will show to better advantage when coupled with good breeding; and that purely natural gifts can be supernaturalized and made the medium of the rarest Christian virtue.

For a Christian, therefore, to set at naught the natural virtues and secular learning is not only wrong but foolish as well. Even in God's own dispensation, the natural is always made the basis of the supernatural. Hence the true Christian policy is not to belittle the natural, which is also from God, but to cherish it and exploit it, and, by directing it towards higher ends, invest it with a supernatural character.

I

Value of Taste for Beauty

It is in view of this splendid teamwork that can be done by culture when yoked with religion, that I do not hesitate to advocate good reading in the home first of all for the purpose of cultivating a taste for beauty. A man may, it is true, love God with his whole heart without appreciating the beauty of an ode by Francis Thompson, a melody by Gounod, a statue by Michelangelo, or a painting by Raphael. But just as philosophy, which is a natural science, deserves to be styled the handmaid of theology; so also taste, or the ability to appreciate the beauties of nature and art, may be made subservient to religion or to the love of God. In other words, if theology is aided by philosophy because the object of both these sciences is truth, of the former supernatural, of the latter natural; then taste, whose object is natural beauty, will be a suitable ally of the love of God, whose object is divine beauty.

Beauty of Virtue

Let me illustrate this by a comparison. A human passion, such as anger, fear, love, is something indifferent, that is, in itself neither good nor bad. If anger is directed towards a proper object and kept within proper bounds, it is something good. It helps to intensify one's hatred of evil. Now a like effect is achieved by the capacity to appreciate beauty. There is nothing in man more beautiful than grace and virtue—than Charity, Faith, and Hope, than purity, humility, meekness; than fortitude in danger, forgiveness of injuries, cheerfulness amid suffering and pain. Hence, the more we have learned to appreciate what is beautiful, the more can our love of virtue be intensified; for by viewing virtue not only as something useful and obligatory but also as something beautiful, we shall have an additional reason for loving it, and we shall strive with greater eagerness to possess it.

As I shall devote this chapter not to a discussion of the beautiful arts in general but only to setting forth the reasons why Catholics should read good literature, the practical question to ask here is: How can a taste for good literature or good reading be acquired? The answer is: In the same way as any other taste is acquired. How does one acquire a taste for oysters or olives? By eating them. The way to acquire a taste for good books is by reading them.

Making Duty a Pleasure

Once a taste for good literature has been acquired, it will be of the greatest help in forming the habit of

good reading; and hence parents cannot begin too
early to cultivate this taste in their children and thus
lay the foundation of the reading habit. To a certain
extent, reading is a duty in our day; and nothing will
make the fulfilling of this duty more agreeable than
the ability to appreciate good books and well-written
articles. It is much the same with reading as with
eating. Few people would likely eat enough to preserve their health, if they had no relish for food.
And even though we eat for the honor of God, as
St. Paul exhorts us to do, it is when we have an
appetite that we derive the most beneficial results
from eating. So, too, it is with mental food. If we
take pleasure in reading, we shall peruse many a
useful book and many an informing article that we
should otherwise not even look at. And even when
we read from a sense of duty, we profit more by
it if it gives us pleasure as well.

Refining Effect of Good Reading

Closely akin to good taste or refinement of mind
is refinement of character; and this, too, is fur-
thered by good reading. The reading of good literature has the same effect on one's character as the
association with good and wise companions. A
writer's best thoughts, most noble emotions, and
finest imagery enter into a good book or good piece
of literature; and the reader's character cannot but
benefit, even though unconsciously, by coming into
such intimate contact with them. The good thoughts
kept in the storehouse of the mind become, sometimes even long after the author is forgotten, the

mainspring of good deeds; the noble feelings strike
a sympathetic chord in the reader's heart and attune
it to lofty aspirations; the vivid pictures leave an
indelible impress on the imagination and thus help
to preserve both the ideas and the sentiments. Even
as a handkerchief that is kept for a time in a per-
fumed casket takes on a delicate fragrance, so is a
man's character sweetened by the reading of good
literature. Especially is this true of books that depict
the lives of great and holy men and women; for in
such books we have in addition to the excellent
thought content the inspiring example of real human
beings who were the very embodiment of the noblest
ideals.

A Splendid Recreation

Nor may we overlook the great benefit that good
reading offers merely as a source of recreation. The
ability to derive pleasure from good reading opens
up avenues of wholesome recreation that would
otherwise remain forever closed. We are so constituted that we must have relaxation of some kind;
yet as rational beings and above all as Christians we
should beware of choosing such forms of recreation as simply kill time. It is an awful thing to
waste time, each moment of which can purchase
the pearl of an eternal reward. And as we shall
have to render an account of every idle word, so
we shall have to give an account also of the use
we have made of our time. Now there is no finer
intellectual pastime than reading; no more entertaining companionship than a good author. It is

true that reading always implies a certain amount of exercise of the mental faculties, and hence work; but what rational recreation does not require activity of one kind or another? Most of our recreations consist essentially in a diversion; not in a change from work to idleness, but in a change from one kind of activity to another: from manual work to mental work or contrariwise; or even from one kind of physical or intellectual activity to a different kind in the same order. Thus a cobbler, who does manual labor indoors all day, finds recreation in doing a little gardening in the evening; while a bookkeeper or stenographer, or even a student, after doing brainwork all day, nevertheless often recreates himself by working out crossword puzzles or writing verses at night. Far from being an objection to reading as a means of recreation, the mental activity implied in reading should rather be an inducement, since it stamps reading as recreation of a high order.

"Movies" No Substitute for Reading

A more subtle objection to reading as a recreation is advanced in our day. So many literary master-pieces, we are told, may now be seen represented by moving pictures that there is no need of reading the originals, since seeing the "movie" affords just as excellent a pastime. Whoever holds such a view labors under a gross illusion. Even if the literary work is only a novel—and hence one of the lowest forms of literary art,—some of the very finest elements are totally lost when it is reproduced as a movie; e.g.: the descriptions of character, the dialogues, the beauties of diction, the various figures of speech, and above all the beautiful thoughts, sentiments, and images in which every truly literary work abounds. Take a moving picture like "Fabiola," which cost an untold amount of labor and expense and was proclaimed to be a picture of exceptional merit. For sheer artistry it stands infinitely below Cardinal Wiseman's great masterpiece from which it is taken. And as for edification, educational value, interest of narrative and charm of character, almost any three successive chapters of the book are worth more than the entire picture. And the same is true of any literary masterpiece. The moving picture most assuredly has its place in the field of education as well as recreation; but it can never fill the place occupied by literature in either of these fields.

Reading for Instruction

As far as the religious life of the home is concerned, by far the most important aim and fruit of reading is instruction. There are laymen who may claim with some justice that their tastes and characters are already formed, and that they do not need to read to improve them; but there is none that can truthfully say that he is beyond the need of instruction. When I speak of reading for the purpose of instruction, I do not mean solely for the sake of learning something new, but also for the sake of refreshing, confirming, and clarifying the knowledge we already have. The storehouse of the mind is the memory; but in our avidity to learn facts, and in our endeavor to acquire knowledge without taking pains, we often stack this storehouse with things in such disorder and confusion that we cannot find them when we want them. In other words we forget. The knowledge really exists hidden away in the recesses of the mind, but we are unable to recall it; or can do so only by dint of long and hard racking of our memory. This shows the truth of the saying that, as regards many things at least, we do not so much need to be told as to be reminded. We must be reminded again and again until the knowledge becomes readily available at our beck and call.

Deepening One's Religious Knowledge

It is true that religious instruction is imparted in church and in the Catholic school; but even supposing the most thorough Catholic schooling and the attentive hearing of a weekly sermon, no average Catholic is beyond the necessity of improving his knowledge of religion by frequent reading. It stands to reason that religious knowledge acquired when the mind is still immature is capable of increase, of widening and deepening as a person grows older. And grown-up Catholics need a far more reasoned and more perfect grasp of the truths of their religion; not only in order to strengthen their Faith amid the dangers of an ungodly world, but also in order to defend it against the attacks of non-Catholics with whom they daily come in contact. For this reason it is important that they be reminded of the truths of their religion not only once a week but daily; that what their pastors tell them from the

pulpit be repeated to them in different form by laymen like themselves; that they learn how to apply
the standard of religion and the moral standards of
the Church to the changed conditions of modern
life and to the new problems that are being dis-
cussed; that examples be frequently placed before
their minds of sterling Catholic men who held Catholic principles and fearlessly put them into practice
in business, in politics, as well as in their profes-
sional, social, and private life; that they be kept
informed of the most noteworthy local, national
and international events affecting the Church; in a
word, that they be kept abreast of the times in all
important Catholic matters.

II

The good results and advantages derived from
reading which I have here set forth, should prove a
sufficient inducement to anyone to cultivate the reading habit, and furnish a satisfactory answer to the
question *why* one should read. Another question, a
question of more practical importance, is: *What*
should we read? My answer will be twofold. We
should *not* read what is dangerous or injurious but
what is wholesome and useful.

Drinking Filthy Water

If a doctor would give a lecture explaining and
praising the highly beneficial effects of the frequent
use of water for drinking, washing and bathing,
none of his hearers surely would understand him to
speak of the use of any but clean and pure water.

The same is to be understood of what I have said of the good effects of reading. The water that we drink and the food that we eat do not more truly enter into our system than what we read enters into our mind. Should we, then, not be at least as particular about what we read as about what we eat and drink? How fastidious many people are nowadays about the cleanliness of their bodies! How much time and care do they not devote to bathing; to removing blemishes; to rendering and keeping the skin soft and smooth! And what vast sums of money do they not spend on fine soaps and creams and powders and other cosmetics, only to keep that corruptible body of clay sweet and clean! And yet these same people, who would shrink with horror from drinking filthy water or from bathing in a polluted stream, do not hesitate to read things that fill the mind with sordid ideas, stain the imagination with filthy images and stir up impure emotions in the heart. The mind can be soiled just as easily as the body. As you cannot touch pitch without being defiled by it, so neither can you avoid besoiling your mind, if you allow it to tread the slippery paths of unclean literature.

Sugar-coated Poison

Nor is the danger of defiling and corrupting the mind to be found only in writings that are pronouncedly immoral or irreligious. Disease germs may prove fatal just as well when taken into the system in wholesome food as when received alone from contact; and poison is poison whether taken straight or with a coating of sugar. There is a vast amount of literature in our day,—books, magazines, newspapers,—that is more or less infected with the germs of moral disease and the poison of unbelief; and it is the more dangerous because the harmful matter is contained amid a deal of harmless matter, or concealed under a false show of humanitarianism, patriotism, equity, justice and the like. We must not forget that all literature, in the main, breathes the spirit of those that produce it; and as the great bulk of literature that appears daily is the product of religiously indifferent, agnostic and wordly minds, it quite naturally breathes the spirit of religious indifferentism, agnosticism and worldliness; and, say what you will, such literature is dangerous to ordinary Catholics because its spirit is contagious.

Source of Unchristian Views

Or whence is it that so many Catholics have decidedly unchristian and worldly views on certain subjects? Without doubt from seeing these views expressed and plausibly set forth, or simply assumed as self-evident, in current non-Catholic writings. The views that Catholic young folk often entertain in regard to marriage and courtship evidently come from this source. Some columnist in a daily paper dispenses advice to lovers, and it is accepted and acted on even though it runs counter to the warnings of confessor and pastor. In like manner another writer devoid of Christian principles descants daily on such weighty topics as evolution, capital punishment, free will, parental authority, self-repression, education, canons of art, the fashion, science and religion; and from the very cocksureness of the author, his dicta are widely accepted just as of old the answers of an oracle.

Unchristian Outlook on Life

To keep your mind sweet and clean and to prevent the purity of your Faith from becoming gradually defiled, I would advise you not to read the popular non-Catholic fiction of the day—the short stories and serial stories that appear in the daily papers and in non-Catholic magazines, as well as most of the non-Catholic novels that have appeared in recent years. I am far from maintaining that all this fiction is wholly bad, or that not even now and then something will appear that is wholly above criticism. The point I am trying to make is that most of this literature reflects an unchristian outlook on life; that the characters it depicts speak and act in a manner that makes this unchristian outlook attractive; and that frequent reading of such literature, just like intimate association with unbelievers, will by and by lead even a Catholic to adopt something of that same outlook and, all unconsciously, allow it to influence his actions.

Bad Company in Fiction

Indeed, in some respects, the mental association with the unchristian and worldly-minded characters in the secular fiction of the day is far more dangerous, because far more intimate, than association with such characters in real life. In real life one's contact with them is usually limited to business affairs, social gatherings, or at the most to private interviews; but in the world of fiction it extends often to the characters' most secret actions and even to their most hidden thoughts. Especially in the realistic stories of our day, there is no sanctum whither the reader is not permitted to follow the characters. He not only associates with them but mentally re-lives their lives, thinks their thoughts, is imbued with their philosophy of life, stirred by their passions, and is a secret witness of all their actions.

There is no getting away from the fact that frequent reading of such literature must, in the long run, have a baneful effect on the reader's mind and character. Hence whoever is in earnest about keeping his mind and heart uncontaminated, will regard the entire field of present-day non-Catholic fiction and popular magazines as outside the range of his reading.

Catholic Periodicals Superior

I admit that this may seem unreasonable to those who have unthinkingly followed the great crowd without observing whither they have gone and whither they are tending. I am even willing to admit that it would be too much to ask you to give up the non-Catholic magazines if there were nothing to offer you in their place. But there is an abundance of Catholic periodical literature not only equally good but better. Mind, I do not say better from every point of view. There may be and no doubt are points in which some Catholic periodicals are inferior; but it is equally true that there are points in which they are decidedly superior, chief among these points being the thought-content, tone and spirit. And since these latter points certainly outweigh any slight advantage that some non-Catholic periodicals may have in point of literary finish, it may be said without hesitation that, all things considered, present-day Catholic periodicals are better than the non-Catholic ones.

Unhealthy Appetites

The great trouble is that the relish for really good reading has to a great extent disappeared; and even many supposedly practical Catholics have got to the point where they no longer care for Catholic writings because the latter lack the sensationalism of the non-Catholic press. This is evident from the class of papers and magazines that these Catholics habitually read. It is not the high-class papers and periodicals that one finds in their homes, but such as appeal to the less noble instincts in man. Nor is it lack of literary excellence that they deplore in Catholic books and magazines. The stock complaint is that they are too dry; that they lack "punch" or "pep" or whatever the current slang word happens to be for that peculiar kind of spiciness which they imagine to be necessary to make a work interesting. But the fault really lies in themselves and not in Catholic literature. It is an unhealthy appetite that is appeased only by highly seasoned food; and such Catholics as have acquired a craving for spicy literary food can set themselves right again only by denying themselves such food and earnestly striving to develop a taste for more wholesome literature.

Choking the Good Seed

Deep down in his heart, I am convinced, every sincere Catholic has a love for the better things in literature. It is an essential part of the Catholic mind. But in many cases this love has not been developed. Like the good seed of the sower in the Gospel, it has been choked by the more abundant and superficially more attractive output of worldly literature. If from early childhood on, parents would allow their children to have only good books and magazines, their children would develop a taste that would endure throughout their adult life. Instead of doing that, many parents bring such trash as the metropolitan Sunday newspapers into their homes and themselves explain the miscalled "funnies" to their children who are unable to read. Doubtless there are many among my readers who have thus, without much fault of their own, become prejudiced against Catholic reading matter. To them I say: Give Catholic reading a fair trial. Select a number of Catholic books and periodicals and determine to read them to the exclusion of all others for one month. If you do that with a good will and an open mind, I feel sure that at the end of the trial you will be so convinced of the superior benefits derived from Catholic reading that your only regret will be that you have been so long a stranger to that wellspring of wholesome thought and noble inspiration.

A Parental Duty

As you are mainly responsible, dear fathers and mothers, for the kind of taste for reading that your children develop, let me urge upon you the duty of providing an ample supply of Catholic magazines, books and papers in your homes. You cannot be content with one Catholic paper or magazine; you should have at least three or four; something of a devotional and something of a miscellaneous character; and something, too, for every member of the family. While many Catholic periodicals have special departments for the young, there are excellent Catholic publications devoted exclusively to juvenile readers, and one of these should be taken by every family that is still blessed with youthful members. And if the subscriptions should seem too expensive, remember that it is a false economy to starve your children's minds while you spend more than is necessary for the feeding and clothing of their bodies. Far better would it be to retrench somewhat on expenditures for creature comforts and fine clothes than to save a few dollars by failing to provide your children with abundant and wholesome mental food. Besides, if you discontinued taking non-Catholic papers and magazines you could easily afford to take Catholic ones.

Good Catholic Books

While it is highly important nowadays to read Catholic periodicals, the very best Catholic thought is ordinarily still found in books—books that are the product of years of study and labor; books that have

stood the test of time and have been handed down
as a precious heirloom to posterity. For a birthday
or Christmas present parents cannot do better than
to present their children with a good book. Start
early by giving a picture book to the children who
have not yet learned to read. And let them be beautiful books, well-bound so that they will last; and
thoroughly wholesome and edifying, so that they
will be worth preserving. If you would make it a
rule to give each child one book a year, a very
respectable family library would gradually be established that would be a source of pleasure as well as
of instruction for many years. A great advantage of
a book over a periodical is that the book can more
easily be preserved and will be read again and again;
and thus its contents finally become part and parcel
of the reader's mind.

Not Only Story Books

In purchasing books for the home or for their
children, let parents not imagine that only books of
an entertaining nature are suitable. They should
occasionally make them a present also of books of
a more solid character—books of instruction on the
truths of our holy religion; books dealing with the
moral problems of the present day; books of piety
and devotion that explain how even the laity can lead
a life of perfection and of closer union with Christ.
There is a vast amount of such popular religious
literature in existence, and it is daily growing more
extensive. Nor is the cost such as would prevent
any ordinary family from having a goodly supply in

its home. While good Catholic story-books may also edify and indirectly also improve one's religious knowledge, it is mainly books that deal expressly with religious and moral subjects that are the main helps which parents should avail themselves of to inculcate in their children the principles of truly Catholic conduct and solid piety.

III

The Best Place for Reading

There remains yet one more question to answer: Where should we read? I answer, in the home. While persons who must travel far by street-car or by train to their place of work can profitably employ the time in reading, the home is usually the best place in which to do one's principal reading. To be able to read with understanding and profit and even with pleasure, a certain amount of leisure and quiet is necessary, and this can mostly be had at home. I speak from experience when I declare that the presence of children does not necessarily interfere with home reading. I was one of the three youngest children in our family, and although we were normally noisy, our parents used to read practically every evening. Sometimes we would be occupied with our school tasks; sometimes we would be playing; and as years went by we usually formed part of the reading circle ourselves. For a mother who has several small children the problem is less easy; but the children do sleep sometime, and then is the mother's opportunity. Can she not take up a book or magazine while putting the baby to sleep? And could she not even keep the children quiet by half reading half narrating a story to them?

Why Mothers Should Read

This is one of the main reasons why mothers should not neglect to read; namely, to be able to instruct and entertain their children. Stories from the life of Christ; the biographical parts of the Old Testament; the lives of the saints afford an endless source of excellent matter for the entertainment and education of the young, and it would be a pity if any mother, from failure to refresh her memory by reading, would be unable to turn this source to good account. When the children themselves are old enough to read, it is important that the parents set them a good example; for if the parents themselves do not read Catholic literature, they can hardly expect their children to do so.

Supervision Necessary

This brings me to another reason why reading should be done in the family circle. It is a strict duty of parents to watch over the reading of their children, and not only of the younger ones but of all that are in the household; and such supervision cannot be exercised unless the children do their reading where their parents can see them. As in most other things, so also in the choice of reading matter, children of school age are unable to decide what will be good for them, and hence their parents must make the selection for them. But even the older children must be watched lest they borrow or buy books or magazines the reading of which would do them great harm. Many a wayward youth was started on the downward path by the reading of bad literature. Hence it would be seriously sinful negligence on the part of parents not to exercise a careful censorship over the reading of their children.

Theodore Roosevelt's Example

Besides exercising great vigilance to keep improper literature out of the hands of their children, fathers and mothers should also make a free but discreet use of their parental authority to induce their children to read certain books or articles that are of special importance to them and to demand an account of their perusal. A very fine practice is to have a child read a short piece, say one of Aesop's fables, and then give it in its own words, or to learn a few lines of poetry by heart. The late President Theodore Roosevelt tells in one of his letters, written while he was in the White House, that, on one occasion when his wife was absent, he had to take her place, listen to the children recite a poem and award them a nickel in case they knew it well. This custom might well be imitated by Catholic parents. Even if the pecuniary award be omitted, the children will be amply rewarded by the benefit they derive from the practice. But they cannot be expected to do such things of their own accord. Play has more attraction for them than reading or learning by heart, at least until they have acquired a taste for more intellectual pastimes.

Hence their parents should accustom them to devote some time every day to good reading, and they will thus acquire a habit that will be to them a source of much joy and many blessings.

The Home Reading Circle

The last reason I wish to mention why reading should be done in the home, is that it serves as an additional reason for staying at home and thus fosters home life. Like family prayer, the family reading circle should be a cherished institution in every Christian home. How happy and easy are the hearts of those parents whose children, large and small, are gathered with them around the library lamp, each one intent on his or her own book, paper, or magazine. Knowing that what the children are reading is wholesome (for they will tolerate only such reading matter in the home) they know that they are usefully occupied; and their hearts will not be racked with anxiety, as is often the case when the children are absent from home.

For the same reason, parents should not allow their children to frequent public libraries and reading rooms. Apart from the grave danger of their reading harmful literature in such places, the practice also tends to disrupt home life. The home is the proper place for the children to read as well as for the principal reading of all the members of the family. When one member of the family is at the theatre, another at his club, a third and a fourth out joy-riding, it is quite natural that the others (if there be any) will be tempted to neglect their reading also and seek amusement elsewhere than in the home. It were well, therefore, if several evenings a week were set aside especially for the home reading circle, so that at least on these evenings each one would profit by the presence and good example of the others.

Preserving Old Books

And let me say a word in favor of keeping old books in the family and handing them down from generation to generation. Many a one who gave away his picture books, scrap-books and nursery rhymes when he grew up, has later regretted that he no longer possessed those books for the entertainment of his own children. So I say, let the books remain in the family, and let each one take his or her books along when the children leave their parents to found new homes. The books would sometimes need to be bound anew; but it would be an added delight for the little ones to know that their father or mother had paged the same books in their childhood; and the parents or grandparents themselves would undoubtedly find great pleasure in viewing again with the little tots the selfsame picture books and illustrated nursery tales that charmed them when they were small.

Yes, how we were charmed by beautiful stories, beautiful pictures, beautiful toys when we were small! Then the whole world seemed beautiful. But how drab, how commonplace it appears to us now. How full of evils it is, and how deeply do we deplore our powerlessness to do away with them.

A Paradise of Books

Yet there is a world from which we can banish all these evils—the world of books. Or rather, by cautious elimination and judicious selection from the plentiful material on hand, we can fashion for ourselves a little world, aye, a little paradise of books in our own homes. And thither we can repair daily to enjoy its pure and bracing air, its lovely change of scene and the delightful companionship of its distinguished men and women. Happy we if we have builded for ourselves such a literary garden of Eden and habituate ourselves, like our first parents, to walk therein with God. We cannot, it is true, see His face or hear the sound of His voice; yet He will oftentimes speak to us none the less distinctly through the medium of the printed page;—raising our thoughts above the petty affairs of daily life, broadening our outlook, correcting our views, calming our fears,—in a word, throwing a glow of Heaven's light and peace on the things of earth, and thus heartening us with brighter visions to take up anew the tedious tasks of this workaday world.

CHAPTER V

Harmony in the Home

WHENEVER two or more persons are engaged in an undertaking, the importance of harmony for success is universally recognized. Thus if two persons set out on a tour by boat and plan to do their own sailing or rowing, they must agree as to the management of their craft, the route to be taken and their destiny. Otherwise their projected tour will be but the occasion of endless contentions and difficulties, will get them nowhere, and perhaps even end in disaster.

The Married Couple's Destiny

Such precisely is the situation of a young married couple that has launched out on the sea of matrimony. By most solemn vows, they have bound themselves to make the journey through life together. But what is the destination of that journey? What is the nature and purpose of the marriage contract into which they have just entered? What duties devolve upon them by virtue of that contract? What attitude must they take on the question of having children? And in the event that they have children, what obligations have they towards them, and how are these obligations to be fulfilled?

Superficial Harmony

These are questions which every serious-minded couple must be ready to answer, and on which they must be in substantial agreement, if they wish to

live in peace and happiness and make a success of
their wedded life. I say, if they wish to make a
success of their wedded life; for they might live
in harmony and attain to a certain measure of
earthly happiness even without agreement on the
aforementioned questions,—but only at the cost of
the real success of their state of life. Thus they
might get along in harmony if they agreed to disregard entirely the question of life's destiny and of
a future life. In like manner, they might get along
harmoniously if, despite decided views or convictions on certain questions; e.g. that of the artificial limitation of the family, one of the two would
yield in all practical points to the will of the other.
That would be harmony on the surface, harmony
in practice, harmony through compromise or even
the abandonment of principle, but not that complete, deep-seated harmony of thought and action
flowing from the acceptance of the same principles
in all essentials, which should be the desire and aim
of every Christian husband and wife.

There is no need of perfect agreement in non-
essentials; and it is doubtful whether complete accord in every particular would even be desirable.
For, while a similarity of tastes and talents, of
aversions and hobbies might add to the harmony of
wedded life, a difference of likes and dislikes in
some things offers a better opportunity for the one
to supplement the other.

Any couple that accepts the teachings set forth in
the foregoing chapters and adopts them as a form
of life will, I am sure, enjoy in its home the

blessing of harmony in fullest measure. Yet, as
there are two kinds of disharmony fraught with very
especial danger to the family, which are nevertheless quite frequently disregarded, they may well be
made the subject of a most emphatic warning and
a more extended instruction.

A United Front

The first of these is disharmony, or the lack of
unity, in the exercise of parental authority. Children are obliged by the fourth commandment to
honor and obey their parents; and parents are required by that selfsame commandment to train their
children to become men and women of character
and virtue. But if children are to obey, there must
be an understanding between the persons who issue
the commands; and if the father and mother are to
train their children, they must agree as to the object
and method of training to be pursued. Self-evident
as this principle must appear to every thinking person, it is nevertheless a principle that is often disregarded in practice. The foundation on which the
training of children must rest is parental authority;
but if that authority is at odds with itself because
of opposition between the persons in whom it is
vested, the entire fabric reared upon it will be weak
and unsteady. In their joint relations to their children, as the divinely constituted bearers of domestic
authority, parents must invariably present a united
front. Whatever differences of opinion, of personal
likes or dislikes they may have, in their dealings
with their children these differences must recede into

the dark background; so that the children will not even suspect that any such disagreement exists, and in consequence will not be tempted to play one against the other or to appeal from the one to the other.

A Second Helping of Pie

To illustrate by a very common example how easily this principle can be violated, let us suppose that the family is seated at table and little Johnny asks his mother for a second piece of pie. Since he had declined to partake of some other more wholesome but less savory foods, his mother very properly answers, "No". A little later, taking advantage of his mother's absence in the kitchen, Johnny repeats his request to his father, who replies: "Here, you can have my piece, Johnny. I don't care for it anyhow." By acting thus, the father definitely takes sides with the boy against his mother; weakens her authority; neglects an opportunity of training his child; and sows the seed of discord between himself and his wife. The circumstance that the father gave his own piece of pie to his boy does not change the situation. The mother did not refuse the lad's request from a desire to economize by saving a piece of pie, but from the desire to train him to habits of self-control and Christian moderation.

A Mutual Understanding

Instances of this kind that call for co-operative action on the part of the parents are of almost daily occurrence in families where there are children. Being pleasure-loving like all human beings and as yet too young and inexperienced to value the merits of self-abnegation and restraint, children are everlastingly begging to have this or that, to go here or there, to be permitted to enjoy this or that diversion or amusement. And not only young children present this domestic problem; the problem persists as long as the children are subject to the authority of their parents, and often calls for the most cautious handling when the growing boys and girls have become adolescent sons and daughters. In every stage of the problem, the only proper policy for the parents to adopt is to present a united front wherever the children are concerned. There must be a distinct mutual understanding that one will support the other, and that all important permissions granted to the children by one parent are dependent on the consent of the other. "We will see what mother thinks about it"; "Did mother say you might?"; "I must first talk it over with father" are standing replies which parents will ever have ready if they are bent on promoting the welfare of their children and maintaining harmony in their home.

Strengthening Mutual Love

By thus upholding each other's authority in the presence of the children, father and mother not only increase their children's respect for their parents and each other's influence with the children, but also knit still more firmly the bond of mutual love that makes husband and wife one moral personage. For each single reference to the other's authority is a gracious acknowledgment of the other's equal rights and responsibility in the marriage partnership, and a tacit renewal of the wedding day agreement to live as two souls with but a single thought.

Nor will it suffice for the one parent to uphold the other in word while at the same time making no secret from the children that he or she would much rather side with them. It would be hardly less harmful, for example, than open hostility for the father to say: "I'm awfully sorry; but you know how mother is. It's useless for me to say 'Yes' when she says 'No'."

The Chief Disciplinarian

Right from the beginning, therefore, there should be an agreement between the parents on all important questions that concern the management and education of the children. And when new problems arise, or when the parents disagree as to how best to apply their principles to certain practical cases, they should discuss the matter out of hearing of the children; and only after coming to an agreement should they inform the children what they have to do. Usually the regulation of most disciplinary matters pertaining to the domestic circle is best left to the mother. She is with the children much more than the father and is less likely to yield to their ill-advised pleadings from selfish motives. The father, returning home from a day's work, is often just as much in a mood to enjoy his children as they are eager to enjoy him; and, unless he is guided by the mother's wishes and rules of discipline for the children, he is very apt, from sheer paternal affability, to undo all the mother's efforts in training the children, make her feel bad, and perhaps even discourage her efforts in the future. For that reason, before conceding the youngsters any privileges on his return home, he should inquire of their mother how they behaved themselves during the day; whether a ride or walk in a park or some other treat would be in order; and the like.

For father and mother always to take each other into consideration, always to stand together like the two pillars of an arch, is to make family life infinitely more agreeable, to share equally its burdens and responsibilities, and in truly constructive fashion to further the training of their children. But if the parents disagree and the children become aware, as they soon will, that they can cajole the one parent into siding with them against the other, then parental authority will be sadly weakened, and domestic harmony will soon give way to a state of tension, then to ill-concealed dissension, and at last to open strife.

The Head of the Family

In case the parents cannot come to an agreement in private on a particular question, then it is the duty of the wife to submit to her husband, so long as no violation of moral or religious duty is in-

volved; for St. Paul says: "Let women be subject
to their husbands as to the Lord; because the husband is the head of the wife, as Christ is the head
of the Church" (Eph. 5, 22). Oftentimes, however, it would be wiser for the husband to yield
to the wishes of his wife when there is no principle at stake; and better still perhaps, if the matter
does not call for immediate settlement, to seek the
advice of the pastor or of some other God-fearing
and experienced friend.

Main Cause of Disharmony

The other kind of disharmony that calls for a
special warning is disharmony or the lack of unity
in religion. It is easy to understand how many of
the difficulties of maintaining harmony in the home
are removed or lessened, when husband and wife
are united by the profession and practice of the
true Faith. And by the same token it should be
easy to understand that, apart from serious character defects or moral lapses in one of the parents,
there is no more frequent cause of dissension and
discord in the home than the lack of unity in religion. Yet many Catholics fail to realize this fact,
and in consequence make the attempt, which nine
times out of ten is doomed to failure, of rearing
the stalwart structure of a truly Catholic home on
the cleft foundation of a mixed marriage.

A Lawyer's Sad Experience

The following quotation from a letter published
in "Our Sunday Visitor" gives the experience with

mixed marriages of just one single lawyer; but it will no doubt open the eyes of many of my Catholic readers.

"As an active practicing lawyer in Chicago, handling divorce cases along with my general practice, I have had considerable opportunity to make investigation as to the causes of domestic strife leading to divorce among Catholic clients where either party married a non-Catholic; and I am now forced to inquire of you what is being done, if anything, to prevent mixed marriages by Catholic men and Catholic women.

"I ask this question only after having handled approximately five hundred divorce cases and cases involving annulment and separate maintenance, wherein one of the parties was of the Catholic Faith; and wherein I have found that this difference in religious belief was fundamentally the cause of almost all of the discontent, sorrow, and trouble which led to divorce or separation; and that in ninety percent of the mixed marriage cases, the Catholic was confronted with the question of abstaining from receiving the sacraments and living with the spouse, or of separation, in order to be able to follow the teachings of our Faith on the matter of marriage duties and obligations."

A Basic Disagreement

But why does a mixed marriage almost inevitably sow the seed of discord in the home? Because the Catholic party accepts and is obliged to accept the teachings of the Church as the only true standard of moral and religious conduct in every phase of life; whereas the non-Catholic party does not accept that standard. From the very outset, then, there is a basic disagreement concerning the most important thing in life. From the very ground up there is a breach between husband and wife, which no unity of sentiment in other things will ever be able to fill. For, no matter how kind, how considerate, how loving, how free from prejudice, how magnanimous the non-Catholic partner may be, the Catholic spouse that has a truly Catholic mind must forever realize most keenly that, so long as the religious barrier exists, there can be no complete understanding of each other, no full and perfect sympathy; because the things that mean most and are most conducive to happiness for the one mean little or nothing in the life of the other.

Complete Harmony

How much more intimate the union between husband and wife who share the same religious convictions! Arm in arm they go to church; side by side they assist at Mass; and together they seek the consolation of Confession and the spiritual nourishment of Holy Communion. In their attitude towards the question of having children, in the choice of a school, in the questions regarding prayer in the home, Catholic reading, courtship and marriage, religious vocation, and many similar matters, the Catholic couple are in complete accord, because these questions are all decided for them in advance by the teachings of Holy Mother Church.

Innumerable Dissensions

What a rift on the other hand in the life of a couple who do not share the same Faith! What one cherishes and esteems, the other perhaps abhors. What one looks upon as an act of virtue or even as a most solemn duty, the other may despise as silly superstition or a mere idle ceremony. Supposing the mother to be the Catholic party to the marriage, which is the more common case, how keenly will she not feel the lack of religious harmony if her husband insists on unnatural limitation of the family; if he objects to having their children baptized by a Catholic priest; if he insists that three or four years' training in a Catholic school is enough to fulfill his promise to have his children brought up Catholic; if he refuses all money for Catholic books, papers and periodicals; if he objects to all display (as he terms it) of religion by means of Crucifixes, pictures of the saints, or other religious articles in the home; if he discourages prayer at meals and all family devotions; if he protests against sending the children to Mass when the weather is the least bit inclement or disagreeable, or against sending them from home without breakfast when they wish to receive Communion; if he scolds about his sleep being disturbed or having to get his own breakfast when his wife goes to early Mass; if he demands meat at all meals on Fridays and all days of abstinence; if he encourages as broadening, the association of his boys and girls with the children of his own Protestant or even irreligious relatives and

friends; if he refuses to call the priest or even denies
him admission into the house when some member of
the family is seriously ill; if—to put an end to the
list—he does any of the thousand and one different
things like these that other non-Catholic husbands
of Catholic wives have done in the past and are still
doing to-day.   For these are not purely imaginary
cases such as everyone must admit might happen.
They are actual cases drawn from stories of mixed
marriages in real life.

The Pre-nuptial Pledge

But some young lady who is contemplating a
mixed marriage may say, on reading the foregoing
paragraph, that she would make adequate provision
against all such possible evil consequences by de-
manding a solemn promise of her future husband
never to interfere with her or her children's practice of religion.   In doing that, she would be doing
only what thousands of Catholic girls have done
before; for the Church requires such a promise as
an indispensable condition every time she tolerates
a mixed marriage.   But it is notorious how lightly
these pre-nuptial pledges are broken, and how sadly
these thousands of Catholic wives of non-Catholic
husbands have been disillusioned when the time
came for the promises to be redeemed.   To make
a promise and to keep it are two quite different
things.   In many cases, too, the non-Catholic party
never had any intention of keeping his promise; or,
if he did, he maintained afterwards that changed
circumstances gave him the right to change his mind.

So it may very easily happen that not many moons have passed since the honeymoon before the wife finds obstacles placed in the way of the performance of so simple and fundamental a duty as the hearing of Mass on Sunday. And even should the wife be gifted with such exceptional strength of character and devotion to her Faith as to practice her religion in defiance of her husband, what would become of domestic harmony?

Children of Mixed Marriages 3/27/2023

Yet even more deplorable than its effects upon domestic harmony will be the effects of a mixed marriage on the education of the children. As set forth in the first chapter of this book, the religious education of the child should begin in earliest childhood, even in infancy, by surrounding the impressionable young heart with an atmosphere of religion, and instilling into its daily expanding intelligence the idea that nothing in this world matters so much as the love and service of its God and Creator. But how can a uniform and lasting impression of this kind be made on the child, when its father and mother, whose combined actions create the atmosphere of the home, are not in agreement on the importance of religion? Certainly, if the mother is not a Catholic, the child will stand little chance of receiving any religious education before it is sent to school. But even if the mother is a Catholic, the child's religious training will be one-sided; because it will lack the support of the father's good example.

Exceptions are Few

Some mixed marriages, it is true, do turn out well, apparently, despite the initial handicap to religion and domestic harmony that ordinarily attends them. But it must be admitted that those are exceptions. The preponderating testimony of experience is against mixed marriages as the cause of loss of interest in religion or of complete loss of Faith on the part of the Catholic consort or of the children.

Something Often Overlooked

But there is still another objection to mixed marriages, the explanation of which will, I trust, make my unmarried readers still more determined never to contract a marriage that would introduce disharmony into their future homes. Very many Catholics, I dare say the great majority of them, are of the opinion that a Catholic is forbidden to marry a non-Catholic in much the same fashion as he is forbidden to eat meat on Fridays, namely, merely by a positive law of the Church; and that the only practical difference between a Catholic marriage and a mixed marriage lies in the fact that the latter may not be celebrated in church nor without a dispensation. That idea is entirely wrong. The eating of meat is not wrong in itself, and the Church has never condemned the eating of meat; but she condemns mixed marriages and abhors them not only as dangerous to the Faith of the Catholic party and the children, but also because entering into such a marriage involves the participation by a Catholic and a non-Catholic in the same sacred rite.

This is a point that many Catholics do not know or entirely overlook. They know quite well that they are not allowed to take an active part in a Protestant religious service; and that to assist as bridesmaid or groomsman at a Protestant wedding is forbidden under mortal sin. Yet the degree of a bridesmaid's participation in a wedding is small compared with that of the bride herself; because, for a Catholic, marriage is a sacrament, and the bride and groom actually administer the sacrament of Matrimony to each other, the priest being only the Church's official witness. It is this intimate commingling in a religious rite by a Catholic with a heretic which is the reason why the Church does not permit a mixed marriage, except for a grave reason, even if it were certain that this or that particular mixed marriage involved no danger to the Faith of the Catholic partner or of the children.

Communication with a Heretic

It will give the reader a better idea of how the Church detests the active participation of her children in a sacramental rite with a heretic, if we observe how she legislates regarding it in other cases. Such a communication with a heretic occurs also when a Catholic receives sacramental absolution or Holy Communion from a validly ordained but heretical priest; and so averse is Mother Church to such an act that only in danger of death does she permit a Catholic to request absolution and to receive

Holy Communion at the hands of such a priest. It is evident, therefore, that there must be a grave reason for permitting any religious communication of that kind with a heretic; and that holds also for participation with a heretic in the Sacrament of Matrimony.

Permitted Only for a Grave Reason

This is another point that is commonly overlooked or not understood. A Catholic must have a grave reason for entering a marriage with a non-Catholic; and a dispensation for such a marriage may be granted only for a grave reason. It is not enough that the couple want to get married and are willing to sign the pre-nuptial pledges. By no means. The first requisite is that there must be some weighty reason for permitting an exception to the general law of the Church forbidding mixed marriages. Only when serious ground for making such an exception exists, may a dispensation be granted,— and even then only on the further condition that the usual promises regarding the practice of religion be given in writing.

The Church Not Too Severe

From the foregoing explanation, it should be abundantly clear to any Catholic that the Church is by no means unreasonable or too severe in her opposition to mixed marriages. To adopt any other attitude would be for her to underrate the sanctity of Christian matrimony, which Christ raised to the dignity of a sacrament, and to underestimate the preciousness of the Faith, which it is her duty to preserve and propagate. And as all those who are so fortunate as to be blessed with the priceless gift of the true Faith are obliged to take the same attitude as the Church on all questions of Faith and morals, the attitude of the Church towards mixed marriages must be the attitude also of all her loyal children.

No Lofty Idealism

It follows, therefore, that in asking you, dear reader, to accept the Church's position on mixed marriages as your own, I am not making an appeal for anything extraordinary or heroic. There is no lofty idealism, far beyond the reach of ordinary mortals, in taking such a stand. It is nothing but plain Catholicism. Any other attitude is unchristian and opposed to the teaching of our holy Faith. That a Catholic should woo and wed only a Catholic is not a sublime ideal, which the Church expects to see realized only in her most perfect children. The marriage of a Catholic with a Catholic is the general rule for all; the only truly Catholic union; the only union the Church positively sanctions and approves. Every other conjugal union that a Catholic enters into, no matter how securely braced with excuses, cautions, and dispensations, is at best only tolerated, —tolerated as a lesser evil, either to right some wrong already done or to avert some impending greater evil.

The Chief Occasion of Mixed Marriages

I trust that every young man and every young woman who reads what I have here written, will be so deeply impressed by the undesirableness of mixed marriages as to resolve not only never to contract a mixed marriage but also to avoid the chief occasion that leads to such a marriage; namely, the companionship of non-Catholics. To mingle freely in a social way with non-Catholics and to say that one is earnestly determined never to marry a non-Catholic is like paddling down the rapids of Niagara with the determination not to strike a rock. The Catholic youth or maiden, therefore, that is in earnest about avoiding a mixed marriage will make no dates with a non-Catholic and accept no invitations to non-Catholic social affairs.

Falling in Love Not Inevitable

But what if a Catholic falls in love with a non-Catholic? A Catholic should not fall in love with a non-Catholic! There are persons, it is true, who maintain that falling in love is something that simply happens and is entirely beyond a person's control; but such an idea of love is opposed to reason and to common sense. Human love is not merely a passion that bursts forth spontaneously upon the perception of a suitable object. It is also a voluntary activity of the will; and hence it is subject to the control of the will, which can check and even extinguish a passion for a person whom one's reason declares to be an undesirable or even impossible partner in marriage. Or is it not this consideration that prevents the poor hired man from falling in love with the daughter of his rich master? Is it not the consideration of the impossibility of a marriage that prevents many a one (not all, alas!) from falling in love with a person already married or bound by the vow of virginity or celibacy? Why, then, should the consideration of the evils of a mixed marriage not suffice with the grace of God to prevent a Catholic from falling in love with a non-Catholic? No, even though the human heart is a strange and wilful creature, it is not so intractable that, with due precautions, it cannot be restrained from desiring forbidden fruit. Hence the Catholic boy or girl who starts out with the correct Catholic attitude that mixed marriages are forbidden fruit, and who does not court danger by mixing socially with non-Catholics, will keep from falling in love with a non-Catholic without extraordinary difficulty.

Conversion of the Non-Catholic Partner

And now a word also to those of my readers who have contracted a mixed marriage and who are still living with a non-Catholic partner. No matter how unpleasant the reading of this chapter may have been for you, you must not be disheartened. You cannot, it is true, alter the past; but you can do a great deal to mend matters for the future. Whether your marriage has been one of those exceptional ones that have turned out well despite the lack of harmony in religion; or whether it has further corroborated the wisdom of the Church in condemning such unions, your duty is the same: you must endeavor to bring about the conversion of your partner to the true Faith. It was with the

understanding that you would fulfill this duty that
the dispensation for your marriage was granted. But
even if Canon Law did not stress this obligation,
you should nevertheless be solicitous for your consort's conversion for his, or her, own sake, no less
than for the sake of religious harmony in the home.

Prayer Alone Not Sufficient

But how can this most desired event be brought
about? By earnest and persevering prayer; by the
constant force of your own good example; by oc-
casional invitations to read Catholic literature and
to attend Catholic services and sermons; and—not
to be forgotten!—also by prudently intimating, on
opportune occasions, your own great desire that
your non-Catholic partner embrace the true Faith.
You must not expect Almighty God to do everything. In dispensing His graces and especially the
blessing of the true Faith, He makes use also of
human means and human agents. And the most
natural as well as the most suitable agent He could
employ to convert your partner in marriage is your-
self. Why, then, this timid reticence on the subject
of religion? If you persist in depending exclusively
on prayer, you may be held responsible for your
consort's long delayed conversion and for his or
her loss of innumerable priceless graces. Such was
the woman who on the day of her husband's conversion exclaimed to him: "This is the happiest day
of my life. I have been longing and praying for
this day for many years." To which her husband
replied: "That is strange. Then why did you never

intimate to me that you longed for me to become a Catholic?"

Enthronement of the Sacred Heart

Among the supernatural means of obtaining the conversion of a wife or husband, one that I would recommend most strongly is devotion to the Sacred Heart of Jesus; and in particular that form of this devotion known as the Enthronement of the Sacred Heart in the home. This consists in setting up an image of the Sacred Heart with appropriate solemnities in the home, and in consecrating the family to the Sacred Heart in permanent recognition of His Kingship over the home. The fruits of the Enthronement have been simply marvelous in all parts of the world. Men who had never gone to Confession in their lives, high-degree Freemasons, have humbly made their Confession after the Enthronement had been performed in their home at the request of a wife or daughter.

To all, therefore, whose home life is marred by the lack of unity in religion or by any other kind of disharmony, as well as to those who wish to preserve the harmony that has hitherto prevailed, I say: Invite a priest to perform the act of Enthronement in your home. Consecrate your family to the Sacred Heart of Jesus. Renew that consecration from time to time, especially on the first Friday of each month; and in the spirit of that consecration regard the Sacred Heart as the King and intimate Friend of your family. Make Him the confidant of your joys as well as of your sorrows, your failures as well as your successes. Let Him be your support in trial, your comfort in sorrow, your refuge in distress. Let His principles govern your family life as well as your private and public life; and then you, too, most assuredly, will realize the truth of those loving promises which the Sacred Heart of Jesus revealed to St. Margaret Mary Alacoque:

"I will bless the houses wherein the image of my Heart shall be exposed and honored.

"I will give peace to their families.

"I will give them all the graces necessary for their state.

"I will shed abundant blessings on all their undertakings.

"I will comfort them in all their trials."

CHAPTER VI

Necessity of Home Life

THE enemies of religion and in particular of the
Catholic Church often maintain that the Church
has failed in her mission to make men virtuous,
because even among Catholics there are many that
lead immoral lives. And some go even so far as to
see in this a proof that religion is incapable of
making men moral. The fallacy of such reasoning
lies, of course, in ascribing to religion those moral
failures who disregard her precepts and who neglect
to use the means of practicing virtue that she
enjoins. The same fallacious reasoning is used in
regard to the home. The home has failed, it is said,
to take care of its members during their leisure
hours; it does not offer recreational facilities
enough, especially for young people. And as our
young people will seek diversion and amusement in
improper places if we do not provide wholesome
entertainment for them, we must have Catholic
clubs and social centers where they can recreate
themselves in a harmless manner.

A Matter of Training

Those of our social workers and sociologists who
reason thus evidently overlook the fact that there
is an endless variety of not only innocent but also
beneficial amusements that may be had in the home;
and furthermore that it is just as possible, by proper
and timely education, to educate people to seek their

recreation mainly at home, because of the priceless advantages that home life offers, as it is to induce them to patronize Catholic community centers in preference to the more alluring public places of amusement.

Such, then, is the purpose of this chapter—to ripen the conviction in the reader that home life should be cultivated on principle by every member of the family; since home life is an indispensable means of obtaining in full measure the blessings of religion in the home and the true happiness and welfare of the entire family.

I

A Plain Duty

In every perfect society, it is the duty of the members to further the purpose of the society. Now the family is a perfect society, whose object is to promote the temporal and above all the eternal welfare of its members. Hence it is the duty of each member of the family to do his share towards the attainment of that end, even at the cost of some sacrifice or of some inconvenience to himself. No member of the family has a right to shirk his duty toward the rest. No member of the family stands alone and is simply free to live his own life without any regard for the others. But the proper fulfillment of each one's respective duty towards the other members of the family necessarily demands the spending of a certain amount of time at home in the family circle.

The Parents' Part

Upon the father, as head of the family, naturally devolves the first duty of fostering home life by his example as well as by providing reasonable recreational facilities, and, if need be, also by using his authority to prevent unreasonable or excessive gadding abroad. Yet, though the father has the greater authority to safeguard home life, the mother, as the mistress of the home, has the greater opportunities; and hers, therefore, should also be the chief care in fostering a deep-seated love of the home and binding all members of the family by invisible ties to the paternal hearth. Indeed, the mother is the real center of attraction, the very heart of the Christian home. Because the care of the children and the superintending, if not always the actual performance, of the household tasks requires her presence, the home is the mother's natural abode, and, with but rare exceptions, her ordinary sphere of action.

A Mother's First Care

It is true, the practice of many women and mothers of our day seems to indicate that women have a much wider field of action than that circumscribed by the limits of the household. Yet that does not alter the fact that woman's natural place is the home, and that, ordinarily, she should not engage in any work, not even of a social or political nature, incompatible with the performance of her duties to her family.* As the great Jesuit authority

*See quotation on page 56.

on moral philosophy, Victor Cathrein, says: "To give her children a good education and to maintain a well regulated household, must always be woman's first care." And lest it be thought that this is an outworn doctrine that must be rejected because of changed conditions, and that woman must needs adapt herself to the times, he continues: "Far from estranging her more and more from this mission, as it must be regretted has hitherto been done in consequence of modern industry and modern ideas, one should aim to regain for her in its entirety the place that she occupied in former times. The foundation of domestic happiness is a virtuous, pious, diligent woman, who loves order, and who possesses the gift of making her husband attached to his family and of educating her children to be good citizens and good Christians" (Moral Philosophy, Book II, p. 384-5).

Exceptional Cases

It cannot be denied that there may be circumstances in which individual women may very properly widen the field of their activities, either for their own advantage, the advancement of women's interests, or for the welfare of the public in general. But these will be, for the most part, women without families, or such whose children no longer need a mother's care; and with women thus circumstanced I am not here concerned.

But if woman's chief concern is the proper education of her children and the care of domestic affairs, her presence in the home is indispensable. Or how can a mother fulfill her sacred duties towards her young children if she is rarely with them? If she is frequently absent from home or if she leaves the children almost entirely in the care of a nurse or maid, how can she guide their childish steps aright, mould their tender hearts to virtue, and administer the necessary admonitions, reproofs, and punishment? For the words of Holy Writ are still as true as they were of old: "The rod and reproof give wisdom; but the child that is left to his own will bringeth his mother to shame" (Prov. 29, 15).

Big Brothers and Sisters

In as far, too, as the assistance of the older children may be helpful or necessary in the care of domestic affairs, the mother not only may but should require it. The training of the children is indeed the mother's duty; but just because it is her duty, she has the right to demand the assistance of the elder children in order that that duty may be properly performed. She has the right to demand that they remain at home to help her take care of the younger children, to aid them with their tasks, or merely to keep them company and entertain them so that they will be content to remain at home. Why is it that sometimes even the very young children are anxious to get away from home, except that most of the other members of the family are out and the children are deprived of the companionship they crave? It is above all at nighttime, and in particular for the adolescent boys and girls, that the home is truly a haven of safety to shield them at least for a time from the dangers of the outside world; and parents may become guilty of grievous sin, if they are grossly negligent in keeping their children at home at night to shield them from evil companions and other occasions of sin.

But even for the elder children, home life is a necessity for the proper development and safeguarding of their spiritual life; and this all the more if they are old enough to be obliged to work and are in consequence exposed to the evil influences of the outside world. Or, indeed, how can they benefit by the practice of family prayer, if they do not take regularly even one meal a day with the entire family when grace is said in common, and if they are never at home in the evening to join in the recitation of the litany or rosary? How will they devote any time to Catholic reading, and how can they be beneficially affected by the Catholic atmosphere of the home, if almost the only time they spend there is spent in bed?

Weakening the Family Circle

But the frequent absence of the elder children from the family circle not only deprives them of the benefits of family prayer, good reading, and a Catholic atmosphere, but deprives also the other members of the family of the benefit of their company and their good example. By absenting themselves from home, they weaken the family circle and make it harder for the rest to profit by the advantages of the Catholic home. If the older children would stay at home, it would be easier for the rest to stay and devote a little time to family prayer and Catholic reading. Their very presence, their interest, and their example would make home life more agreeable, and all would become more and more permeated with the wholesome influence of a Catholic atmosphere. But if one brother or sister goes out, another will want to go, too; if the elder brothers and sisters are gone, the children will not wish to remain at home; and thus the family is broken up and instead of a place to live in the home becomes merely a lodging and boarding house—a place where one sleeps and perhaps takes one or the other meal.

Modern Conditions No Excuse

No matter how common this state of things is at present or how well satisfied people may be with it, it is greatly to be deplored; and parents as well as children should do their utmost to restore the home life of the family to its pristine and normal condition. Every member of the family should be prompted to foster home life for his own advantage, because it is for his own good to spend the greater part of his time at home. He should be further impelled by regard for his brothers and sisters, whom he is bound to love more than others not so closely related, and whom he should be willing to help by his company and good example. And lastly he should be induced by love and gratitude towards his parents, when they desire him to remain at home; and even by obedience, if they direct him to stay at home to take care of the children, to help them with their tasks, or merely to entertain them.

The parents themselves are in duty bound to foster home life, because it is an almost indispensable means for the proper Catholic rearing of their children. It is the presence of the parents, and especially of the mother; it is their example, their authority, their interest, and above all their love that must knit the family together, ward off the dangers that threaten it from without, breathe into it the true Catholic mind and Christian spirit, and guide it to its eternal destiny.

It is the Home That Counts

This old-fashioned doctrine has recently found champions in unexpected quarters—the camp of the psychiatrists—as may be seen from an article entitled "Home Still in Fashion," in "The Literary Digest" for October 10, 1931. Commenting on an address to 2000 school principals in New York by Dr. Leon W. Goldrich, director of New York City's newly established Bureau of Child Guidance of the Board of Education, the New York Times says that it has been demonstrated that any home, even one of contention and unkindness, is better for the child than no home at all. "It is a doctrine which until recently demanded exceptional courage to maintain. An age devoted to self-expression and freedom preferred to think of the harm done by taboos and fixations, and to overlook the good done by fathers who provided food and shelter and mothers who provided care." We are now emerging from this revolt against the home, continues The Times. "People are beginning to say generally in print what the social workers and the officials of the juvenile courts have been saying all the time . . . . It is the home that counts. Scientists are beginning to emphasize the importance of loving care—the very thing recently abominated as the source of so many complexes."

It is almost needless to say that I do not advocate spending all one's leisure time at home, nor maintain that one must never go away except for very urgent reasons. There may even be homes in which the moral conditions are so bad that it would be more advisable to spend the majority of one's evenings away from home. But apart from such very exceptional cases, one may safely say that home life is not fostered as it should be by those persons who, without sufficient excuse, spend the majority of their evenings away from home.

II

The Causes of the Trouble

If people are to be interested in the great social work of making the home circle flourish once more, it is necessary for them to understand the causes of its disruption. One of these, the expansion of industry, has already been alluded to; but as the purpose of this book is to bring about an improvement of the Christian home even before the reform of our present industrial system may be hoped for, it will be more to the purpose to expatiate on other causes; and chief among these, without doubt, is the inordinate quest of earthly pleasure.

Joy versus Pleasure

In that charming little book, "More Joy," by Bishop Paul Wilhelm Keppler, the author points out the important distinction between joy and pleasure. There are too many pleasures, he says, and too little joy. Which is only another way of saying that too many people seek happiness in things that are not conducive to true happiness; and consequently, though they give themselves up to amusements, to the enjoyment of sensual pleasures, they do not find true joy but merely a temporary forgetfulness of life's burdens and sorrows. True joy consists in contentment, in peace of heart, in the testimony of a good conscience, in the control of one's animal instincts by reason, in the subjection of the passions. Man being a rational and moral being, albeit an animal, cannot find real joy in pleasures that conflict with reason and the moral law. And that is why those people are most joyous who are content, for the most part, to find the needed recreation in the simpler joys of the family circle. For these joys are consistent with a good conscience, whereas the pleasures that are the usual offering of public places of amusement can frequently not be indulged in without either searing one's conscience or at least exposing oneself to grave moral danger.

The Lure of the Gang

If I should be asked to state in particular what pleasures tempt different members of the family to spend their evenings away from home, I should say that in the case of young men, and especially those still in their "teens," it is mainly the pleasures found in the company of the "gang." By the gang I do not mean a number of boys who are usually found together in their outings, nor the boys of a neighborhood who are regular playmates in their daily games. Such gangs hardly interfere with, and oftentimes practically coalesce with the family circle. No, the gang that seems to me to be a menace to home life and to the proper training of young men, is a group of boys who usually spend every evening and the entire evening together at some place away from their homes; and I do not hesitate to call the desire of a boy always to be with "the gang" an inordinate desire for pleasure and a dangerous occasion of sin. For what is the chief attraction of such company? The absence of all restraint. They want to be alone with youths of their own age, unobserved by their parents or teachers. They want to enjoy liberty, independence; and this liberty consists in freedom from all restraint—from the restraint of cultured society, the restraint of politeness, the restraint of gentlemanly deportment, the restraint often even of Christian virtue and common decency.

Bad Influence of the Gang

But freedom from such restraint cannot but have evil consequences for undeveloped characters, as experience proves only too well. Where is it that vulgar words and expressions are most commonly heard? In the company of the gang. Where is it that indelicate stories are unblushingly told? In the company of the gang. Where is it that obscene hints are given, suggestive remarks made, improper songs sung? Where is it that gambling is learnt, drinking taught, disobedience, untruthfulness and dishonesty towards parents and teachers approved and applauded? In the company of the gang. It is the almost uninterrupted daily association with such company in such circumstances that roughens the character and degrades the morals of our young men. And the most natural and most effective means of withdrawing them, at least to a great extent, from the debasing influence of such company, is to have them spend the majority of their evenings at home in the company of their mothers and sisters. The naturally more gentle and more refined nature and manners of mothers and sisters are a splendid means of leavening, of tempering, and of toning down the coarser and wilder nature of the young man and the growing boy. And happy the boy and the young man who submits to the influence of such companionship! That companionship, coupled with the entire influence of a good Christian home, will go far towards saving him from the evils of the "gang."

Girls' Sets and Parents' Clubs

No less disastrous than the gang in disrupting the family circle is the girls' set as well as father's and mother's clubs. The objections to be made against the girls' set, unless its gatherings are far less frequent and properly chaperoned, are the same as those I have made against the boys' gang. It opens the door to unrestrained liberty and contempt of time-honored conventions for which the less respectable element among our modern young womanhood is so justly condemned. As to the clubs to which the parents and especially the mothers belong, nothing craves more wary walking than these. Many a child is a stranger to parental care and to all the blessings of home life because of its mother's insane devotion to her club, or to what she dignifies by the name of "social duties." There are wives and mothers who imagine themselves bound to be busy almost everywhere except in their own homes. One afternoon or evening they must be at their club; another afternoon, at a card party; another day, they must attend an afternoon tea or a lecture; and still another day, a reading or sewing circle. And thus, what with their social calls and social duties, they are mostly absent from their homes and their own children are neglected.

Charity Begins at Home

If such mothers would only devote themselves conscientiously to the God-given task of bringing up and training their own children instead of attending, or even giving, lectures on the uplift of society, society would be in a far better way than it is at present. It may be that some of these women are at heart well-meaning and sincere, and that, blinded by the glamor of altruistic activities, they do not realize their mistake. But the truth of the matter is that the performance of welfare work is often an excuse for neglecting the more confining and more tedious household duties. No matter how good and praiseworthy it is to practice the corporal and spiritual works of mercy, our Lord certainly would not countenance a woman's practicing them to the neglect of her own family. A woman's first social duty is to her own family. Let that duty be properly attended to first, and then she may think of extending her charitable activities abroad. Charity should begin at home.

Value of "Movies" Overestimated

A second attraction that draws not only the young men and the young women, but even their younger brothers and sisters away from the home at night, is the theatre, and especially the moving picture theatre. A great deal may be said in favor of the "movie," not only on account of its recreational but also on account of its educational value; yet it is my opinion that this value is greatly overrated, and that, as far as children are concerned, whatever amount of education may be obtained by attendance at moving pictures can be equally well obtained by other means. In other words, I firmly believe that a child that never attended a "movie" can, and in most cases will be, just as well educated as one that attended "movies." It would be possible to show that whatever good is accomplished by the "movies" (and I am speaking only of the good ones), is discounted by the harm that they indirectly do even to the cause of education. But as I am speaking now of the "movie" only in its relation to the home, I wish to emphasize here merely this harmful result of attendance at the "movies," that it withdraws the members of the family from the sanctuary of the home, and by developing the "movie" habit, makes it impossible for them properly to share in the beneficial influence of Christian home life. In view of the fact that children lose nothing worth while by rarely attending moving pictures, and that frequent attendance almost inevitably withdraws them from one of the best of all educational influences, that of a good Catholic home life, it is hard to understand how thoughtful parents can be so imprudent as to take their young children regularly to such amusements even before the latter are old enough to attend school. But such parents usually reap the fruit of their folly. If children become accustomed from early childhood to frequent public places of amusement, it is not surprising that in their adolescence they can hardly be restrained from roaming about at night.

Excessive Joy-Riding

The third great enemy, and no doubt the greatest enemy, of home life in our day is the automobile. As long as practically the whole family goes riding, and as long as the outings are not too frequent, there is no objection to this means of recreation, in particular for those families who are thereby enabled to benefit by the advantages of a more healthy atmosphere and a more agreeable environment. Yet it cannot be denied that the thing is overdone. In many families the car is in constant use. The children want to be out at every possible opportunity, and the far more valuable means of recreation to be had at home are neglected. In other families the car is used in turn by different members of the family. One evening it is one of the boys who has it; another evening, one, or perhaps two, of the girls; a third evening the parents, and thus the family circle is always incomplete and it is impossible to enjoy the benefits of real home life. It is imperative, therefore, that parents who aim to promote the true welfare and happiness of their children put a stop to this excessive automobile-riding.

A Snare to Virtue

Though I am speaking here of the automobile only in as far as its use affects home life, it may be useful to add a word of warning to parents against permitting their son or daughter to go riding unchaperoned with a companion of the opposite sex. Not only Catholic priests but also non-Catholic judges and social workers deplore such rides as the occasion of the moral downfall of countless young men and young women. If the boy and girl are honorable and sensible, they will welcome a third person to their party both as a means of warding off suspicion and as a guardian of their virtue. And in order that their adolescent boys and girls may take this sensible view of the matter, parents should instruct and train them betimes to follow Christian and not pagan standards of propriety in their relations with persons of the opposite sex. Unless they do this, their children will almost inevitably take their cue from what they read in secular papers, from what they see on stage and screen, and from what they witness in actual life; and this to their own great moral detriment, to the disedification of their acquaintances, and often-times to the tragic grief of the very parents who refused to be so old-fashioned as to curb their children's liberty.

III

Homes Must Be Made Attractive

What a world of evils would disappear at one happy stroke, and what a world of good would be accomplished, if people would only stay at home and be occupied in the family circle! The great question is, then, how shall we induce people to stay at home? If it is the desire for amusement, for recreation, for companionship, that leads them abroad, how shall this desire, which is certainly legitimate, be satisfied at home? In advocating home life, nothing is farther from my thoughts than the desire to deprive anyone of legitimate pleasure. Indeed, to put more real joy into men's lives, while at the same time furthering their spiritual interests, is the very purpose and object of this book. If I thought that it would not help to achieve this purpose, I would cast it into the fire.

Cleanliness the First Requisite

By all means, then, the home must be made attractive. The attractions that lure one elsewhere must be offset by counter attractions in the home. The strongest tie that binds one to one's home is love of home—a quality that can be developed just the same as the habit of frequenting public amuse-

ments is developed. Therefore, the first requisite
for attracting one to one's home is that the home,
the abode itself, be pleasant and inviting. Even the
humblest home can meet this requirement, at least
in the interior; for poverty does not imply squalor,
slovenliness or disorder. Let only cleanliness prevail, let only the rule be observed, "A place for
everything, and everything in its place," and the
resultant neatness and tidiness will lend a simple
dignity and attractiveness to even the poorest interior. It is by no means always the luxurious or
palatial homes that are the most charming. Cosi-
ness, like hospitality, is more often found in the
workingman's bungalow than in the rich man's
palace. One cannot imagine the Holy Family of
Nazareth living in a splendid home. They were
poor, and their abode undoubtedly reflected their
poverty. Yet, however scanty their resources and
however stinted their use of earthly goods, one cannot but believe that their home was a model of
cleanliness, orderliness, and good taste. For cleanliness is not only next to godliness, as the proverb
says, but actually pertains to godliness when practiced from supernatural motives, as it certainly was
by the Holy Family; and as it easily can be by anyone when practiced for sweet charity's sake. If
God will reward a drink of cold water given in His
name, and will regard what we do to the least of
His brethren as done to Himself; then surely He
will look with approval on the pains we take to
make our home attractive to those with whom He
wishes us to share it.

Ownership of One's Home

It will be readily understood that the married couple that owns its home will be more likely to be attached to it and more inclined to make it attractive. For this reason all young couples should endeavor to own a home of their own as soon as possible. The very fact that their dwelling place is their own will give them a feeling of security and independence that they can never have in a rented home. And when they own the soil beneath their feet; when they need consult no landlord on making improvements; when they have no fear of being forced by the sale of their home to seek another dwelling place, their love for their home will strike firmer roots and quite naturally give birth to the desire to make it harmonize ever more and more with the home of their dreams. Ownership of one's home, too, is the best guarantee against a life spent in restless and ill-advised wandering from place to place. In fine, it is the only surety one can have of enjoying the blessings of a fixed abode, chief among which are a firm anchorage amid the vicissitudes of life, a circle of true and tried friends, lifelong associations, and that peculiar charm which in all civilized nations is associated with the word home. Like the lowly cottage overgrown with ivy, a home may be very plain and prosaic itself; yet to him for whom it was the center of childhood's joys, youth's aspirations, and manhood's struggles and achievements, it will always be beautiful with the clinging ivy of fond recollections.

Effect of Mutual Love

The strongest means, without doubt, of holding the family circle together is the practice of mutual love between all members of the family. The scriptural saying that charity covers a multitude of sins may be fitly applied to the home whose poverty and consequent lack of material attractions is more than compensated for by the unselfish love that pervades it. Just as warm-hearted kindliness can light up and lend charm to even a homely countenance, so it can also brighten a home and by its almost magic influence transform a hovel into an abode of delight. This often explains why many a child finds the far more humble home of a neighboring family more attractive than its own.

Feeding the Fire of Affection

Only too often this congenial atmosphere is wanting in the home, not because the inmates do not love one another truly, but because they do not manifest their love sufficiently. There is a lack of the little courtesies and amenities that are so powerful a means of fostering affection. Even the most sincere and deep-seated affection must be fed, if it is not to wither and fade. It is like the cozy hearth fire which must have fresh fuel now and then, if it is not to burn low or go out altogether. Failure to heap the coals of kindness and sociableness upon the fire of family affection is sometimes due to a naturally sullen disposition. More often it can be traced to lack of training in that point; the parents failed to foster sociableness among their children. Quite commonly it is the result of pre-occupation with other affairs—business, social or private interests. At times, too, it is due merely to oversight. Attention was never directed to the propriety and advantage of cultivating habits of mutual kindliness, cheerfulness, and good will; and in consequence there may be a touch of chilliness and gloom about the home where an atmosphere of genial warmth and sunshine should prevail. But, whatever the cause of deficient sociableness in any members of the family, it can and it should be removed.

Effect of Kind Words

The story is told by the author of "The Man Who Was Nobody" of a man who never thought of saying a friendly word to his wife and family. A friend called his attention to the fact. He made it clear to him just how he was acting and what an effect it was having on his dear ones, even though they never complained. He listened to what his friend had to say and agreed that he was right. He promised to begin to do better that very day. That evening he went home a changed man. He greeted his wife and children; he said nothing about business and the worries of the day; at the dinner table he led the conversation. In every way he was most considerate. After the meal was over he went so far as to put on an apron to help dry the dishes. When his wife saw that, she broke down. "What's the matter?" he exclaimed. "Oh, everything has gone wrong today," she replied, "and to cap the

climax you come home drunk." His conduct was
so affable, so different from what it had been, that
there seemed to be only one plausible explanation;
namely, that he was drunk.

Politeness the Robe of Charity

If any of my readers should be obliged to admit
that their past conduct has resembled that of the
man in this story, they, too, no doubt will decide
to reform. For it needs only that it be pointed out
for one to realize that little attentions, little com-
pliments, little words of appreciation, encouragement, comfort, and cheer are dispensed with as
much propriety within as without the home. To
mention but one instance, should we not have a
cheery good morning, a kind good-bye, a pleasant
word or smile of welcome, and a cordial good-night
for the members of our family just as well as for
our friends and acquaintances? It is quite true that
politeness is not of the essence of charity. As practiced by worldly people it is a purely natural virtue,
and it is sometimes used as a cloak for a very
uncharitable disposition. But it can be supernaturalized, and the fact that it is sometimes mis-
used by evil men is no reason why the good should
disdain it. Because of its exterior resemblance,
politeness might well be styled the garment of
charity. And so well does this vesture become the
queen of all virtues, that charity never appears more
gracious, never shows to better advantage, than
when arrayed in the charming robe of Christian
politeness.

Need of Occupations at Home

Despite the attraction of pleasant surroundings and congenial companionship, the urge to leave home during leisure hours may still be very strong if there is nothing to do at home to occupy one's leisure. Here, then, is another point that calls for attention in making the home attractive; and among the various occupations conducive to that end I would assign first place to the performance of certain tasks or the care of certain things. Let parents begin early to develop in their children an active interest in their home by assigning to each the care of a certain thing and by teaching them to take pride in doing their part well. Thus one could have the bookshelves to keep in order, or the library table; another the dining room table; a third some pot flowers to water, and so on; each one having the care of his own toys, shoes, and other personal belongings. Outdoors, to one could be assigned the care of the lawn or a part of it; to another a flower bed; to a third the walks or the porch; and each one should have a small portion of the kitchen garden to cultivate or at least a tiny patch to weed and water. The keeping of a few chickens or other domestic fowl would offer another interesting as well as useful occupation. And to keep the children from growing one-sided as well as to revive their interest, they could also take turns in the performance of certain tasks, either every day or every week or every month, whichever way might be thought best.

Pet Animals

Then there are the pets—dogs, cats, rabbits, singing birds, parrots, anything that will enlist the interest of the children and serve as another tie binding them to their home. Interest in such things can be developed to such an extent that children will sometimes rather forego some other pleasure than leave home and neglect the things committed to their care. To foster this interest, the parents themselves must show a keen interest in their children's efforts, and always have a kind word of encouragement, appreciation or praise for their achievements, no matter how trivial and childish the latter may be.

Games and Toys

And finally, though most of the occupations I have spoken of really constitute excellent recreation if properly directed and not overdone, there must needs be also sheer amusements—pleasurable pastimes, undisguised enjoyments, and care-free indulgence in interesting games. In these days of the player piano, the phonograph, and the radio, not to speak of the numerous playthings that electricity and other modern discoveries and inventions have produced, this phase of the problem of home life is not hard to solve. But even in those families that may be too poor to afford such luxuries, there need be no lack of amusement; for the old-fashioned games of lotto, dominoes, checkers, mill, cards, authors, and parchesi, all of which may be had for a few cents each, can still hold the interest of old and young alike. By one who has a little skill, many of these games can be fabricated at home with hardly any expense; and the fact that they are home-made often makes them the more enjoyable. Indeed, it is a quite common experience that few games are enjoyed more by children than those that are entirely their own invention.

Not Too Many Inhibitions

There is just one more bit of advice that I think should be given in this chapter and that is: Let there not be too many inhibitions in the home! Those who must guard against excess in this point are the mothers and the elder sisters. It goes without saying that even the members of the family will not enjoy staying at home, if they are not made to feel at home; and no one can really feel at home, if he is hampered at every turn by instructions and reminders not to do this and to avoid that. Discipline and order there should be, of course; but it need not be the discipline and order of the church or schoolroom. The very proximity of the walls and ceiling impose a certain amount of restraint that is absent out of doors; but it need not be the restraint demanded by the presence of strangers. Yes, mother dear, and dear elder sister, train your dear ones in orderliness and neatness and well-bred deportment; but let it be done with the sweet reasonableness of a mother and sister, and not with the tyrannical imperiousness of a Xantippe. If undue restraint is placed on them at home, your growing boys and girls will soon find an opportunity of escaping to more congenial places of amusement; and then, instead of spending your evenings in the midst of a joyful, if perhaps a little too noisy family, you will be left to keep late and lonely vigils worrying over your wandering boys and girls and perhaps over the head of the house himself.

Make Everyone Feel at Home

By all means, then, let the home folks be made to feel at home. Let the father of the house occupy the finest easy chair, even if he is not arrayed in his Sunday clothes. Let the grown-up sons smoke in the sitting room or in the parlor, even if the smoke does stain the curtains or the wall paper. Let there be music and song and games at the time for recreation, even if they are somewhat noisy. Let the children have their own theatricals, if they like to; let there be an abundance of clean wholesome reading matter, picture books, puzzles, and toys; let the parents themselves join in or at least show an interest in the amusements of their children, and the home will become so attractive that there will rarely be any temptation to seek recreation elsewhere.

"Keep the home fires burning" is the slogan I would suggest to all who are laboring for the reform of society. Instead of nightly faring forth to the club, the theatre, the "movie" or some other place of amusement, let the members of the family once more gather round the hearth, whether to work, to study, to read, to amuse themselves or to pray. Better far one such night spent in the bosom of the family and in the atmosphere of a truly Catholic home than a dozen nights spent at the club or the "movie," no matter how unobjectionable, educational and inspiring.

A Voice in the Wilderness

Think not, kind reader, that I do not realize (and oh, how poignantly!) that, in making this plea, I shall be looked upon by the great majority as hopelessly behind the times, and as making a futile effort to turn the current of our modern age. But was there ever a more glorious battle fought for a principle, or was there ever a more heroic stand made in defense of the right than when the defender was faced by overwhelming odds? If, like St. John the Baptist, I am but the voice of one crying in the wilderness, at least I have the consolation of being in good company. And if, like the early Christian apologists who raised their voices in protest against the persecuting emperors, I may seem to be trying to stave off the inevitable, I again find comfort in the fact that the Church that the apologists defended still exists and exerts her benign influence, while the all-powerful empire that persecuted her is long since a heap of ruins.

God's Grace Still Powerful

It is true, the Church is the work of God, and its preservation, its spread, and its conquests have been accomplished more by the power of God than by the wisdom and power of man. But so, too, is the family, and especially the Christian family, the work of God; and if it is to accomplish its God-given mission in the Christian home, it has less need of human means than of divine. And therein precisely lies my hope. God's grace is still active and still powerful; and it is solely through it and not "by the persuasive words of human wisdom," that I hope to accomplish any good through these pages. There are still well-meaning souls in this wicked world; souls who want to do the best they can; naturally Christian souls who long for something better, higher, nobler. It is to these especially, and, more particularly still, to young wives and mothers that I address myself in the hope that, as they read these instructions and counsels, the grace of God will inspire them anew with a strong desire and an earnest determination to make their homes models of what a Christian home should be. Let them establish their homes on the rock bottom of religion; let them cultivate prayer, foster good reading, preserve a Catholic atmosphere in their homes and promote home life, and, by the blessing of God, their homes will become veritable strongholds of the Faith, schools of virtue, abodes of peace and happiness and love, which the angels of God will delight to visit, and which God Himself will look down upon with pleasure and bless with a foretaste of the joys of Heaven.

Conclusion

IT is with a feeling of deep satisfaction that I bring this little book on the home to a close. God grant that it may be the humble instrument of accomplishing at least a small amount of the good for which it was undertaken. To that end I can only beg the kind reader who has had the patience to peruse the foregoing pages, not to put the book aside for good after the first reading, but to pick it up again and again until the lessons it contains become deeply engraven on his heart. The substance of those lessons is this: that since society, which should help the individual to lead a God-fearing life, has become a means of leading him astray, to counteract this evil influence, the family, which is the unit of society, must be reformed by being again imbued with the spirit of Christianity. When religion once more directs, controls, and permeates the family life, not only will the individual have an effective safeguard against the evils of society, but society itself will be reformed.

The means to accomplish this end are the simple but efficacious ones that I have pointed out. Think not lightly of them, dear reader, on account of their simplicity, and despise them not for that they are old. Parents above all, fathers and mothers, see to it that these old-fashioned manifestations of Catholic life once more come into honor in your homes. You cannot have religion without religious exercises, as little as you can have fire without fuel.

Nor can you make of your religion a purely church affair, because it is something that touches life at every point.

To children, and especially to those young men and young women who will soon be looking forward to establishing homes of their own, I say: If you hope to have a truly Christian home when you marry, you must lay the foundation for it now. Be faithful to the practice of daily prayer and frequent Communion in the years of young manhood and young womanhood; be chaste during the time of courtship, and you may justly expect God to bless your future home. But if you neglect your religion and incur the wrath of God by your liberties in keeping company, you run great risk of building your Christian home upon sand. Avoid the occasions of sin, therefore; for he that loveth danger shall perish in it. Let me warn you especially against following that custom, as pernicious as it is widespread, which accords young unmarried couples the privilege of almost as complete privacy and seclusion as if they were already married. The proper place for keeping company is in the presence of the father and mother or some other member of the family. These nightly tête-à-têtes and long drawn out private interviews between two young persons of opposite sex are occasions of sin and a source of many other evils, not the least among which are hurried and unhappy marriages. It is during the time of courtship, I repeat, that the foundation is laid for the future home. Let it be made of religion and virtue, my dear young men and young ladies, and then you can securely build up thereon that beautiful edifice, that bulwark of religion, that fortress of morality, that pillar of society, that citadel of peace and happiness—the model Christian home.

Home, sweet home! What a multitude of tender thoughts and feelings are associated with the utterance of that sweet word! What a host of happy memories it conjures up of the innocent days of childhood, of the carefree days of youth, of the toilsome days of maturer age. The home is, indeed, the center of the sweetest and purest of all earthly joys, the starting point of all that is best and greatest in human history. Our Divine Savior Himself gave the home a special consecration by gracing the humble home of Nazareth with His presence during thirty long years; and He thereby gave us also the first and the supreme model of the truly Christian home. Yes, so sacred is the word home that it is commonly used to designate even that eternal dwelling place that God has prepared for those that love Him.

Love your home, then, dear reader, and try to make it worthy of that sacred name. You can adopt no surer means than to establish religion in your home by enthroning the Sacred Heart as its King and by conforming it as closely as possible to the home of the Holy Family. If the father seeks to imitate St. Joseph; if the mother emulates the loving care of Mary; if the children are docile and diligent after the example of the Child Jesus; and if all seek first the Kingdom of God and His justice,— be it ever so humble, yours will be a happy home. What, then, if those foes of your salvation, the devil and the wicked world, storm and rage without,— you and yours will be safe within the walls of your Christian home. For, built as it is on the rock of Faith, we may truly say of it what Our Blessed Savior said of those who hear His words and do them: "And the rain fell, and the floods came, and the winds blew; and they beat upon that house, and it fell not; for it was founded on a rock" (Mt. 7, 25).